T0147174

God –
the Adults' Imaginary Friend

MICHAEL F. LAWLOR

WESTBOW
PRESS®
A DIVISION OF THOMAS NELSON
& ZONDERVAN

WestBow Press books may be ordered through booksellers or by contacting:

WestBow Press
A Division of Thomas Nelson & Zondervan
1663 Liberty Drive
Bloomington, IN 47403
www.westbowpress.com
1 (866) 928-1240

ISBN: 978-1-9736-7563-1 (sc)
ISBN: 978-1-9736-7564-8 (hc)
ISBN: 978-1-9736-7562-4 (e)

Library of Congress Control Number: 2019914797

Print information available on the last page.

WestBow Press rev. date: 10/11/2019

Contents

ACKNOWLEDGEMENT

It is impossible to remember all the individuals who have had a positive influence on my life. Please excuse me for my limited memory. I will acknowledge the following: First, my Lord and God Jesus. Second, my wife Linda who is a gift to me from my Lord. Third, if not for the friendship of Jim and Carolyn Pounders, I would not have been a Christian or, in anyway, a somewhat educated individual. Lastly, I thank the North Boulevard Church of Christ in Murfreesboro, Tennessee, with whom Linda and I attended in the years of 1973 – 1976.

To all who have had a positive influence in my life I say, "Thank You."

INTRODUCTION

One of my sons, once said to me, "You know a lot about stuff that nobody wants to know about." I have to agree with him 100 percent. Why? In the last thirty years, people, ideas, and thoughts have changed dramatically. The material I will share with you is mostly for my children and grandchildren and for those children after them, not for the general public. I am concerned that if I don't give them this important information, which I know will help them live lives of peace, contentment, and happiness, no one else will.

Today, we often receive our information from electronic media, much of which seems to be opinion, not fact. For example, I've watched television channels like Science, History, National Geographic, and Discovery, and the information they disseminate is not fact but speculation disguised as fact or just lies. The same applies to the slanted news companies, from the way they use the word *evolution*, to the ridiculous way they refer to distance in time and space, to the way they describe anthropology. They never say *might be, could be,* or *we think it could be.* They use the word evolution but never the *theory of evolution.* They say there are one hundred billion stars in the Milky Way galaxy. Is it possible that there could be two hundred billion?

How do they know, when nothing we know of has ever been outside of our own galaxy? They use the word *light-year,* as if there was such a thing. Has anybody or anything ever traveled a light-year? No! A light-year is, they say, about 186,000 miles per *second*! Think about that: 186,000 miles per second. Can anyone truly comprehend that? The Superconducting Super Collider, located on the border of France and Switzerland, cannot—no matter how hard they try—reach the stated speed of light. So is there really such a thing as a light-year?

The media, in every discipline, uses hyperbole to make people believe what they want people to believe. I recently read Michio Kaku's book *The Future of the Mind*. He writes, as a fact, on the first page of his introduction, "There are 100 billion stars in the Milky Way galaxy." His book also includes the following statements:

- "But as we evolved from reptiles to mammals" (18).
- "We will see throughout this book the clever and ingenious devices that evolution has crafted" (35).
- "What were the evolutionary forces that gave us this genetic heritage after we separated from the apes?" (157).
- "This approach tries to follow Mother Nature, which has created intelligent beings (us) via evolution, starting with simple animals like worms and fish and then creating more complex ones" (220).
- "As we've seen, human consciousness is an imperfect patchwork of different abilities developed over millions of years of evolution" (226).

Did he say that there *might be* 100 billion stars in the Milky Way galaxy? Did he say *maybe* we evolved from reptiles? Did he say that it *could have been* evolution that used clever and ingenious devices? Did he say that we *could have* evolved from apes or from simple animals like worms? Did he say *we think* human consciousness developed over one million years? No, everything that he wrote was presented as facts, but his statements are not the truth. I will not let my children or my grandchildren or anyone else be brainwashed. I used Michio Kaku as an example because I have heard him say the same things on several television networks.

A great man and writer Dr. Francis Schaeffer wrote in his book *How Should We Then Live?*:

> There is a flow to history and culture. This flow is rooted and has its wellspring in the thoughts of people. People are unique in the inner life of the mind what they are in their thought world determines how they act.

This is true of their value systems and it is true of their creativity. It is true of their corporate actions, such as political decisions, and it is true of their personal lives. ... People have presuppositions, and they will live more consistently on the basis of these presuppositions than even they themselves may realize. By *presuppositions*, we mean the basic way an individual look at life, his basic worldview, the grid through which he sees the world. Presuppositions rest upon that which a person considers the truth of what exists. People's presuppositions laid a grid for all they bring forth into the external world. Their presuppositions also provide the basis for their values and therefore the basis for their decisions. ... "As a man thinketh, so is he," is really most profound. (19)

To put it simply, if you think something is right, you will accept it as right; an example would be abortion. The decision to legalize abortions was a personal opinion of the Justices of the Supreme Court of the United States, and that decision is still a personal opinion. Another example is homosexuality and what is called same-sex marriage. That decision was also a personal opinion of the Justices of the Supreme Court. It was the personal opinions of five out of nine people.

Do people make the most important decisions in their personal lives by using their own personal opinion or someone else's personal opinion? Yes, they do, and I will give some examples. When some people are very sick, such as having cancer, they may make every decision based on their own opinions instead of the opinions of medical doctors, who have been trained in a specialized field to help them. People also make personal medical decisions for their children. When parents make all the medical decisions for their children without involving the medical community, the result sometimes is the death of that child. Another, example would be the use of money. Would a person who has a substantial amount of money make all the decisions on how to invest or handle that money, using only his or her personal opinion, rather than seeking professional help? Yes, and it happens all the time. Example: people who have won millions of dollars have ended up with nothing in a very short time because they did not seek the advice of a professional—that is according to many documented reports.

Today, people truly believe that their opinions are absolute truth, regardless of what the facts really are. If you listen to individuals on the radio, television, and most other media or even when you have a conversation with someone, you will hear individuals make three statements with regard to making their decisions. After they have used the three statements, on any topic, that is the end of the discussion for them, whether the other person is finished discussing the subject or not. After they have used these three statements, they will walk away; their minds are now closed. Those three statements are as follows:

- That is what I think.
- That is what I believe.
- That is what I feel.

These three statements are the new *absolutes* for all but a few people.

In deep or personal conversations that I have had with others, seldom has the person said to me, "I really don't know the answer to that. I'll do some research and get back to you."

We should ask what gives this person or any person the right to express a strong opinion without at least listening to the facts pertaining to the subject we were discussing. Is this person we are talking to educated and trained in the subject discussed? When I bring my car in to be repaired, and the technician says he has repaired it, I do not question his expertise because I know he has been to school repeatedly to make sure he understands every component of that car. Therefore, I trust his judgment.

Nancy Pearcey, in her book *Total Truth*, coined a phrase that captures the essence of how people think today. She calls it *radical individualism*, with the emphasis on radical. Today, people's thinking has become even more radical. I would add one more word to her phrase; it would read this way: *radical irrational individualism*, with the emphasis on irrational. Today, in what is called postmodernism, people say things like, "Whatever," or "To each his own," or "It's my life," or, as a great singer once sang, "I did it my way!" Such statements mean that the person is telling us, "I do not care what you or any other person thinks. I am going to do and think what I want, regardless of what the facts are."

George A. F. Knight, in his book *Christ the Center*, writes,

> Consequently we hear declared today that we are in a post-Christian era that this is the New Age of Man, and it requires a whole new intellectual approach if we are ever to use the word "God" again. In this "postmodern" age, we have actually gone beyond a mere return to Platonism (which at least had the advantage of being a single coherent view of how things are) but have actually taken up other ancient ideas and decided that there is no longer any overarching worldview. As a result, each of us may have our own faith. The logic of this position is that no one of these individual faiths is right. It is virtually a declaration (usually made quite unwittingly) that there must only be a pluralist approach to reality. The result is that a belief in pluralism has actually become the new religion in itself, despite the widely held view that all individual searches for truth are "valid for me", even if, perchance, they are not right.
>
> Consequently we are told to respect and not deride all those who dabble with Zen, then try Confucianism, take refuge in Buddhism or Indian mysticism, or else in one of the Western cults that have invaded us from the East, such as Theosophy, Spiritualism, Voodooism, Anthroposophy, Astrology, even the examination of the human anatomy and psyche; from the latter it is said there arises a hedonic nativism, perhaps described as "the alternative life style", shown in the sexual revolution, or more radically and specifically in the pursuit of money, power, acclamation-all aspects of the New Age wearing its multifarious and fissiparous face in any and all of these "new religions." (78)

Carl Raschke, in his book *The Next Reformation*, explains radical individualism like this:

> The "postmodern temptation," Groothuis asserted, "is to entice souls to create a self-styled spirituality of one's own, or to revert to the spiritual tradition of one's ethnic or racial group without a concern for objective truth or rationality. "Furthermore, said Groothuis, postmodernism is the same as "nihilism," the fashionable View, emerging in the late-nineteenth century, that there is no supreme or enduring truth other than what anyone arbitrarily wills or chooses that truth to be. "Truth decay is a cultural condition in which the very Idea of absolute, objective, and universal truth is considered Implausible, held in open contempt, or not even seriously considered." (15–16)

C. S. Lewis, in *The Screwtape Letters*, writes (and this is Satan speaking), "I have known cases where what the patient called his "God" was actually located-up and to the left at the corner of the bedroom ceiling, or inside his own head, or in a crucifix on the wall. But whatever the nature of the composite object, you must keep him praying to it—to the thing that he has made, not to the Person who has made him" (30).

As a practice, as you read this material, please do not let the names of the writers bother you. I believe you don't need to know how to pronounce their names; just remember these writers are the brightest and most intellectual writers who have addressed the issues we are discussing. Please just read the quotes.

In volume 2 of *The Ante-Nicene Fathers*, a second-century writer and philosopher named Athenagoras converted to Christianity. He lived in about AD 177, and his books were presented to the Roman emperors Aurelius and Commodus. He wrote in his book, *A Plea for the Christians*,

> For poets and philosophers, as to other subjects so also to this, have applied themselves in the way of conjecture,

moved, by reason of their affinity with the afflatus from God, each one by his own soul, to try whether he could find out and apprehend the truth; but they have not been found competent fully to apprehend it, because they thought fit to learn, not from God concerning God, but each one from himself; hence they came each to his own conclusion respecting God, and matter, and forms, and the world. (132)

The discipline that uses the idea of radical irrational individualism and that uses the words *I think, I believe,* and *I feel* as having absolute meaning is religion.

The idea of religion being what some have called personal and private is a complete and total lie, disguised as an atheistic trick. No religions—and I repeat, *no* religions—are personal and private, although billions and billions of people today hold to this idea. How could a religion be personal and private and have more than one member? (Do not tell anyone I have a religion!) Religion is public and is to be proclaimed. This is one of the biggest problems in our country and the world. This problem is what I call the world epidemic of self-made gods—everyone thinks they are all-knowing and all-powerful in their own minds. I am not alone in saying people think they are self-made gods.

Norman L. Geisler, in his book *Philosophy of Religion,* writes,

But there is a radically immanent, irreligious stance taken by some contemporary men not only because of the inability to discover the Transcendent but also because of an *unwillingness* to make a total commitment (or even a partial one) to it. This unwillingness is the second characteristic of a nonreligious experience. There are many reasons why some men would refuse to commit themselves to the Transcendent, even if it were there: (1) it is deemed unworthy of their devotion, (2) man considers himself mature enough to get along without the Transcendent, and (3) the individual desires to honor himself as ultimate.

In brief, a man may be irreligious or purely humanistic in two ways. First, because he is unable to see a transcendent, and second because he is unwilling to submit to it. In either event, his experience would fall short of being adequately religious. (24)

Geisler also states, "Sartre's designation of the fundamental human project as the desire to be God is an even clearer indication of the essentially religious character of man. To be man means to reach toward being God. 'Man makes himself man in order to be God'" (25).

He quotes Walter Kaufmann this way: "Walter Kaufmann repeats the same point even more dramatically, claiming, 'Man is the ape that wants to be God'" (25).

Much like the idea that religion is personal and private, another idea is that there must be separation of church and state. Where did this idea come from? The statement "separation of church and state" is totally misquoted and misused. For the benefit of all, please allow me to give a brief historical explanation of that statement. As I understand it, a letter was written to President Thomas Jefferson on January 1, 1802, by the Baptist Association of Danbury, Connecticut, thanking him for his strong stance on religious liberty and letting him know that they had some issues about religion within the state of Connecticut. The idea of separation of church and state came from a phrase Jefferson used in his reply, when he said "their legislature should 'make no law respecting an establishment of religion, or prohibiting the free exercise thereof,' thus building a wall of separation between Church & State." From that statement came, the misunderstood and misused statement of separation of church and state.

What are individuals who are religious supposed to do when they walk into a state building? Before they enter, should they stand on the stairs and announce as loudly as they can that they are atheists? Please tell me how to make this separation.

People try to live in a vacuum, and they don't want to be disturbed by anyone, regardless of the consequences. That means they do not care about their grandchildren or about what is happening on their streets, in their communities, or in the country. All they want—as Francis Schaeffer said in his book *How Should We Then Live?*—is "personal peace and affluence," meaning, *Leave me alone, and leave all my money and my stuff alone.* What a mess we have created for ourselves by taking to heart the idea that religion is personal and private and that there should be separation of church and state.

Is there a solution to this religious confusion? Yes, but people need to investigate and to try as hard as they can to look at facts, rather than just answering with "I think," or "I believe," or "I feel" to difficult questions. As we look at many facts about religion, you may obtain an understanding of some things you *didn't* understand prior to our discussion, after we reason together.

One more very important statement: the apostle Paul said, "I am the chief of all sinners." That statement applies to me as well. I certainly do not want you to listen to me; I want you to listen only to the facts. This presentation is about how to unravel some of the misunderstandings of religion and especially Christianity.

Let's begin with the difference between the people I call *Goddians*—a word I created to denote people who believe in God (the majority of believers in the world)—and Christians.

In his book *Bowling Alone*, Robert D. Putman writes,

> Virtually all Americans say they believe in God, and three out of four say they believe in immortality. There is no evidence that these beliefs have wavered over the last half century. The Gallup poll and other survey organizations have asked Americans repeatedly over the decades, "how important religion is in [their] life," and the responses suggest only a modest slippage in this metric of religiosity. However, as one of the leading American religious historians has observed, "Unless religious impulses find a home in more than the individual heart or soul they will have few long-lasting public consequences." (69)

People say that they believe in God, but they can't answer simple questions about their God. For instance, consider the following questions:

- What do you mean when you say the word God?
- Where is your God?
- How do you get to know your God?
- What does your God do for you?
- Does your God love you?
- What does your God teach you?
- Is there any historical information about your God?

If you ask people these questions, they may answer the questions with *I think*, *I believe*, or *I feel*. Why? It's because they cannot give a logical or reasonable answer to the questions. We should all be able to give a logical and reasonable answer for our faith. We all must have a good religious foundation and education.

In his book *Introduction to Religious Philosophy*, Geddes MacGregor writes, "but when all that is said, it is surely evident that it is by intellectual inquiry that we make the greatest advances in a field of human knowledge, and that so important a field as religion needs to be thought about with at least as much skill and care as any other. Confused or naïve thinking about religion leads to just as unfortunate results, to say the least, as does such inadequate thinking in other fields" (11).

He also writes, "So when someone says. 'I believe in God,' or 'I do not believe in God,' he is really telling us practically nothing. We need to know what he means by 'believe' and we certainly need very much to know what he means by 'God,' before we can understand what his position is and what he is trying to say" (13).

When building a house or a large building, you must begin with a strong foundation. A strong foundation is also necessary to live a good life. The way you think also must have a strong foundation, and this foundation will determine the way you make decisions in your life. The foundation must be built on more than your own personal views or political ideas, or by radical irrational individualism, or by unrestricted freedom. If you live in this country and allow very important decisions to be made by the people's majority vote, then let's have a brief discussion about democracy and the will of the people.

Let there be no misunderstanding: I love our country, and I served our country in the military, but a country that is operated by democracy can be a wonderful place to live, or it can be the most awful place to live—and history bears me out. The will of the people is not always the will of the Lord, which in all things should be considered first. We are confident that the best plan of government is to let the majority rule, which is the same idea the Roman people had when they said, "The will of the people is the will of God." This may be true in politics (although I have my doubts about that), but to live in a peaceful and orderly country, the people's worldview—or their philosophy, the way they think—is of much greater importance than the number of people who think a certain way. Many countries that have allowed the majority of people to rule have disintegrated their own country because of how the people thought.

I would like to mention somethings that I believe are the thoughts of the people who are disintegrating our country.

First is that we think we have the freedom to manipulate human life. Today, our country and most other countries are manipulating human life any way they like. The idea of seeing the two substances that create human life as nothing but slime is, in the eyes of our Lord, destroying potential human life. How many pieces of what scientists, doctors, and millions of people call *slime* have already been put together and destroyed? No one knows, but it would be a number that we would not believe if it was considered human life (as it should be). This is not even considering that abortion, the termination of a pregnancy, can be performed in the first month or the ninth month, or just as the thing, a child, has the head out enough so that someone can withdraw the contents of its brain. The thinking of the people and the idea of radical irrational individualism has made this possible. Is the will of the people the will of the Lord?

Second, immorality in our country is on a rampage. Drunkenness, drug abuse, lying, cheating, stealing, adultery, divorce, gang violence, love of money, selfishness, homosexuality, homosexual marriage, transgender individuals, murder, rape, pornography, assisted suicide, child abuse, elder abuse, offensive language, love of animals over love of people, misuse of money—I could list plenty more. Is the will of the people the will of the Lord?

Third, there is apathy, meaning most people in our country do not care unless the things mentioned affects them personally. The voice of the people is not the voice of the Lord!

I, along with my children and my grandchildren, will stand on a firmer foundation than opinion, and our foundation will be filled with peace, contentment, and happiness.

This foundation will not be money and things, although it will be very difficult to convince most people that money does not bring peace, contentment, and happiness into our personal lives. To do so, we need to look at those people who are very wealthy and have everything. Many wealthy people are very discontented with life, using drugs, sex, and alcohol; owning mansions, cars, and every other material thing to try to find peace, contentment, and happiness. For them, life is still an unhappy place. Money and materialism are not a solid foundation to build on. These things are only temporary and do not give peace, contentment, or happiness for very long.

Now let's get back to Goddians (my word for those who believe in a God but do not have any basis for that belief). Most people cannot answer the simplest questions about God or the Bible. For example, when people were asked, "Who was Noah's wife?" most answered Joan of Arc. Today, people do not want to use their intellect when it comes to the subject of religion, so for a change, let's look at the subject of religion with facts.

Part 1

A Brief Understanding of God the Father

Let's look at the definition of God the Father from many well-educated individuals to help build a strong foundation for our lives. This information will provide a very brief but (I hope) sufficient understanding of God the Father. When I refer to God, I am referring to God the Father. You know—the Big Kahuna, the man upstairs, our Father who art in heaven, the main man, God bless America; I think you get the idea. Today, the word God has become just another generic noun. A few quotes may be helpful to understand God the Father.

CHAPTER 1

God the Father Is Just a Phrase

FRANCIS A. SCHAEFFER, A WELL-KNOWN writer, theologist, and twenty-first-century philosopher, authored *He Is There and He Is Not Silent*. In this book, he wrote the following:

- "Let us notice that no word is as *meaningless* as is the word 'God.' Of itself it means nothing" (13–14).
- "The mere use of the word 'god' proves nothing" (14).
- "Modern men are trying to find answers just in the word 'God' in god-words" (34).
- "Previous mysticisms always assumed something was there. But modern man's mysticisms are semantic mysticisms dealing only with words; they have nothing to do with anything being there but are simply concerned with something in one's own head, or in language in one form or another. The modern taking of drugs began as one way to try to find meaning within one's head" (48).
- "Today it is linguistic analysis almost everywhere in the world" (48).

C. S. Lewis, in his book *The Screwtape Letters*, wrote that Satan, when speaking to his workers, said, "We have taught men to say, 'my God' in a sense not really very different from 'my boots'" (81).

Today, not only is the word *God* used as a noun, but his name is also used as slang. In his book *Philosophy of Religion,* Norman L. Geisler wrote, "Let us always be cautious." British Anglican bishop Ian Ramsey warns "of talking about God in straightforward language. Let us never talk as if we had privileged access to the diaries of God's private life" (244).

Geisler wrote,

> Only the Tetragram (YHWH, Yahweh) indicates God's true essence and its meaning cannot be known. It denotes "absolute existence" but this can be known only negatively as that that which cannot not be. In brief, God can be understood only in terms of His own essence and no man can know the essence of God. God's Name is peculiar to Himself. The best men can do is safeguard its transcendent unity by negating all plurality from it.
>
> Thus, negative theology is the only protection of monotheism. Despite the fact that Maimonides refers to God as Wisdom and Absolute Existence, he has no positive conception of what these mean. God has no intrinsic causal relation to His creatures and, hence, cannot be named from perfections found in them. What God is essentially must remain unknowable except negatively. (264–265)

Geisler also wrote, "God-Language is richly anthropomorphic; God is beyond all our inadequate pictures and concepts" (302).

CHAPTER 2

God the Father Is Transcendent

WHEN ANYONE THINKS ABOUT GOD, the first word that one should think of is *transcendence.* What is transcendence? *Baker's Dictionary of Theology* by Everett F. Harrison defined it as a

> theological term, referring to the relation of God to creation. It may mean (1) difference or otherness distance or remoteness. In the OT EX. 24; Isa. 6:1; 40:12–26; Ezek. 11:22–23 God's transcendent holiness and glory is compatible with his gracious presence. He is the holy one in the midst (Hos. 11:9), independent and different from his creatures (Isa. 55:8–9), yet near in providence and grace. (Ps. 139). (528)

In *Philosophy of Religion*, Geisler described transcendence like this: "It is that Beyond, beyond which one seeks no more beyond" (16).

In the book *Introduction to Religious Philosophy*, Geddes MacGregor wrote,

> The claim of religions is that their object (God) is beyond experience, so that when religious people talk about God they are, by their own admission, talking about something of which they have no experience. They are talking of what "transcends" experience, and of its very existence, therefore, they can no more meaningfully talk than I can pretend to tell you whether

the King of Ruritania takes sugar in his tea. Certain religions, notably Judaism, Christianity, and Islam, lay special stress on the "transcendence" of God. God, they say, is so completely other than the world of ordinary experience that it is only in a very special sense, and due, *for example, to God's own act, that I am able to "know" anything about him at all.* (23)

MacGregor also wrote,

That God should be so incomprehensible is not surprising. We have seen already how mysterious I must be to myself, and though according to the theist man becomes less mysterious when God is postulated, it does not follow that God is thereby made more comprehensible. At the most we may expect only to have what might be called a faint glimpse of the divine as mediated through our relationship to God. (149)

F. F. Bruce, in his book *The New Testament Documents: Are They Reliable?*, wrote, "God in his divine essence and attributes, God who cannot be directly known" (39).

James W. Sire, in his book *The Universe Next Door,* wrote, "*God is transcendent*, this means God is beyond us and our world. He is *otherly.*" He also wrote, "God is immanent, here, everywhere, in a sense completely in line with his transcendence. For God is not *matter* like you and me, but Spirit" (25). Sire also wrote, "Of course God himself is forever so beyond us that we cannot have anything approaching total comprehension of him" (30).

J. N. D. Kelly, in his book *Early Christian Doctrines*, wrote,

Philo taught that God is utterly transcendent; He transcends even virtue, knowledge and absolute goodness and beauty, the eternal Forms which his revered master, Plato had postulated. God is pure being, absolutely simple and self-sufficing, and can be described as without quality which probably means that, by His transcendence, He cannot be included in any of the logical categories in which we classify finite beings. (9)

This information is extremely important if you are to have a proper understanding of God the Father. After a few more quotes, you will be more educated about God the Father than most people are today. The people I am quoting are well educated in the matters we are discussing. You will see names of individuals who may not be familiar to you, but just read what they have said. Most of these writers lived in the first, second, and third centuries. Some of these writers witnessed Jesus personally, and others were companions of the apostle Paul, the apostle Peter, or the apostle John. One of the writers, Clement, has his name written in Philippians 4:3, and the apostle Paul says, "His name is written in the book of life." He was with Paul. I hope that you, like me, will be interested in what he has to say.

I want to stay away from opinion and give as many facts as possible from some of the best and most educated in this area. We are at the beginning of developing a foundation.

Novatian, a great leader of the early church, wrote two books that we know of: *De Trinitate* and *De Cibis Judaicis*. He wrote what I would call the best book on the Trinity. We don't have much personal information about Novatian. His books are extremely impressive, and that says enough about this great Christian man. He wrote, "God is above all things Himself containing all things, Immense, Eternal, transcending the mind of man; Inexplicable in discourse, loftier than all sublimity" (612).

Justin Martyr was a man after my own heart. Book after book has been written about Justin Martyr. As I read his books, I was elated to know that he was like any other man who wanted to know how to find peace, contentment, truth, and happiness for his life, and he pursued his endeavor through honest, intellectual means. According to all the sources I have read, he was considered one of the most intelligent and well-educated men of that time.

At one time, a great intellectual named Plutarch said that Justin

Martyr surpassed Plato in his thoughts on divine justice. He was a Samaritan, whereas most of the early Christian writers were Jewish. He wrote to the emperor of his time and explained to him the unmerited persecution of Christians, and because of his letter or book, Christian persecution was eased. He opened public schools and taught theology. It gives me sorrow to say that because he would not sacrifice something to the Roman gods, he was put to death.

We will start a discussion about God the Father after the following quote from Justin Martyr. He wrote in *The Dialogue of Justin with a Jew,*

> These and other such sayings are recorded by the lawgiver and by the prophets; and I suppose that I have stated sufficiently, that wherever God says, 'God went up from Abraham, or, 'The Lord spake to Moses, and 'The Lord came down to behold the tower which the sons of men had built, or when "God shut Noah into the ark," you must not imagine that the unbegotten God Himself came down or went up from any place. For the ineffable Father and Lord of all neither has come to any place, nor walks, nor sleeps, nor rises up, but remains in His own place, wherever that is, quick to behold and quick to hear, having neither eyes nor ears, but being of indescribable might; and He sees all things, and knows all things, and none of us escapes His observation; and He is not moved or confined to a spot in the whole world, for He existed before the world was made. How then could He talk with anyone, or be seen by anyone, or appear on the smallest portion of the earth, when the people at Sinai were not able to look even on the glory of Him who was sent from Him? And Moses himself could not enter into the tabernacle which he had erected, when it was filled with the glory of God; and the priest could not endure to stand before the temple when Solomon conveyed the ark into the house in Jerusalem which he had built for it? Therefore, neither Abraham, nor Isaac, nor Jacob, nor any other man, saw the Father and ineffable Lord of all. (263)

CHAPTER 3

God the Father Is Incomprehensible

GOD THE FATHER IS INCOMPREHENSIBLE. He cannot be seen, and he cannot be heard. He cannot be touched. He cannot be talked to directly. Everyone seems to have a false understanding about how to communicate with God the Father. Today we hear statements such as, "I pray to God"; "I know God has saved me"; or "May God bless you." We hear preachers and ministers of all types telling people what God said or what God wants, inferring that they have direct communications with God the Father, but that idea is extremely misleading and harmful. The idea of people directly knowing God the Father is a laughing matter, and it can do serious mental damage to many people.

I believe absolutely that God the Father exists. As we proceed with our discussion, and you read of such great men as Justin Martyr, my explanation should become clear. Kate Bowler wrote a book titled *Blessed*. In that book, she tells of many people and preachers who used the idea of God to make other people think that they had a special and a more personal relationship with God than anyone else. And they used the word *God* in a way that makes others think that they know exactly what God the Father thinks and wants others to do with their lives.

Bowler writes,

> Osteen chose mainstream language over Christian jargon, changing the term "positive confession" to "positive declarations. Yet the principle remained the same: change your words, change your life. He wrote:

"Every day, we should make positive declarations over our lives. We should say things such as, 'I am blessed. I am prosperous. I am healthy. I am talented. I am creative. I am wise.'" For Osteen, the transformative power of positive confession could be demonstrated psychologically, rather than appealing to the forces of faith. The words build self-image, Osteen taught, for "as those words permeate your heart and mind, and especially your subconscious mind, eventually they will begin to change, the way you see yourself." A healthy mind became an important indicator of good spiritual health and a vibrant conduit of faith. Life's circumstance still depended on a believer's use of faith. Divine wealth eventually will come to good people, he reasoned, for a chain of causality- linked thought, the spiritual self, and life's circumstance. "As you speak affirmatively, you will develop a new image on the inside, and things will begin to change in our favor." God rewarded the faithful with wealth, though believers earned it indirectly. Perhaps a careful budget tamed household spending or the boss noticed believers' cheerful attitude and tapped them for promotion." If you'll do your part God will do His," promised Osteen. "He will promote you; He'll give you increase, but first you must be a good caretaker of what you have." Promotion and increase arrived as an assortment of ordinary and supernatural opportunities. A believer should simply rely on God's promise of an abundant life. "Call in what God has promised you," Osteen urged readers." (125–126)

Geddes MacGregor, in his book, *Introduction to Religious Philosophy*, writes,

A Unitarian speaker, Dr. Davies, has more recently put it this way. He said of contemporary American experiments in "religious" enterprise: "What we are seeing is not spiritual regeneration but mass hypnotism. It recalls the techniques of advertising. Like the radio or television announcer: 'Try God, folks. He will clear away your troubles in a twinkling. Works for you while you sleep … Try God! This program is brought to you by Self-Interest and Vulgarity, Incorporated.' "And again: he writes, "Most of those who think themselves religious are really atheists … they *think* they believe in God. But what they truly believe in is their own prosperity, deified; their own happiness, their own advantage … As soon as their prosperity is shrunken … they feel that God is *doing* them an injustice." (29)

An example of this is a television commercial for a pillow. A man says that his *pillow* was a "godsend." This is not an extreme example. Not long ago I was watching a documentary in which an old man was flying an airplane in Alaska. The airplane was about to crash, and the man said, "Right then and there, I prayed to God." He thought because he was going to die, he'd better call directly to God the Father for help. The idea that all anyone needs to do is call out to God, at any time, and God the Father will hear them is wrong. This thinking is not only in our country but in the world—and remember it is the thought pattern in a person's brain that is of the greatest importance and that is the predominant thought pattern about God the Father.

God the Father is *beyond* beyond. Let's read more from the best-educated and brightest people in this discipline.

In *Ante-Nicene Fathers*, volume 2, Theophilus writes to Autolycus. Theophilus was known as one of the earliest commentators. He took the four Gospels—Matthew, Mark, Luke, and John—and explained them so others could understand and respond to their teachings. He was also known as the earliest Christian historian. Theophilus was a follower of Justin Martyr and of the great writer Irenaeus. Read what he has to say about God the Father. Theophilus wrote, "The appearance of God is ineffable and indescribable, and cannot be seen by eyes of flesh. For in glory He is incomprehensible, in greatness unfathomable, in height inconceivable, in power incomparable, in wisdom unrivalled, in goodness inimitable, in kindness unutterable" (89).

Volume 5 of *Ante-Nicene Fathers* contains "A Treatise of Novatian Concerning the Trinity." Novatian wrote, "God is Above All Things, Himself Containing All Things, Immense, Eternal, Transcending the Mind of Man; Inexplicable in Discourse, Loftier Than All Sublimity" (612). He also wrote the following:

- "He [God] has no time" (612).
- "We can in some degree be conscious of Him in silence, but we cannot in discourse unfold Him as He is" (613).
- "How can we by possibility conceive how we may grasp these very things? —we shall mentally grasp what God is, if we shall consider that He is that which cannot be understood either in quality or quantity, nor, indeed, can come even into the thought itself" (613).
- "Moreover, He is Good, Always the Same, Immutable, One and Only, Infinite; And His Own Name Can Never Be Declared, and He is Incorruptible and immortal" (615).
- "Whence it results that God's own name also cannot be declared, because He cannot be conceived" (615).
- "He is therefore also both immortal and incorruptible, neither conscious of any kind of loss nor ending. For because He is incorruptible, He is therefore immortal; and because He is immortal, He is certainly also incorruptible" (616).
- "For that which *is*, according to what it is, can neither be declared by human discourse, nor received by human ears, nor gathered by human perceptions. For if "the things which God hath prepared for them that love Him, neither eye hath seen, nor ear hath heard, nor the heart of man, nor even his mind has perceived" (616).

Volume 1 of *Ante-Nicene Fathers* contains the writings of Irenaeus against heresies. Irenaeus wrote several books to combat heresies; he wrote to correct those who were misrepresenting true Christianity, mainly those who thought they had a special and superior knowledge above all others.

Irenaeus wrote, "But in respect to His greatness, and His wonderful glory," no man shall see God and live, for the Father is incomprehensible" (Exodus 33:20) (489).

People have been using God's name as if he is available at their beck and call. As I've mentioned, I saw a TV ad in which the individual said that his pillow was godsend. (Please, God, I need a pillow. Help me!) How utterly ridiculous to try to communicate with God the Father for such a frivolous thing. That is where we are when it comes to understanding God the Father. I do not like using the word *ignorant*, but that's the only word that truly describes the misunderstanding of people today with regard to God the Father. People are ignorant; they have a complete and utter ignorance of God the Father. Ignorance is Satan's clandestine plan; it's always been his plan to confuse people's understanding of God the Father.

C. S. Lewis was a great and accomplished man. He wrote thirty books that were published in thirty different languages. He sold millions of books around the world. He wrote *The Chronicles of Narnia*, *The Screwtape Letters*, *The Space Trilogy*, *Mere Christianity*, and *Miracles*, to name a few. *The Screwtape Letters* is written from Satan's perspective. In one scene, one of Satan's subordinates writes to one of his own workers—a person that Satan is trying to control—and says, "Give him a grand general idea that he knows it all and that everything he happened to have picked up in casual talk and reading is the result of modern investigation" (21). He also tells him, "As always the first step is to keep knowledge out of his mind" (44).

Geddes MacGregor, in his book *Introduction to Religious Philosophy*, writes, "Moreover, such are the defects in contemporary education that a man might nowadays attain high international standing as a biologist or chemist though he knows no more about the elements of religious thought than medieval pope knew about the quantum theory" (333).

We have more information about the Christian religion than any other generation has ever had in almost two thousand years, yet people do not even bother to obtain factual knowledge about religion or even their own faith. People make decisions not based on facts but on the basis of what religion they like or enjoy or what makes them feel good. Willful ignorance is something anyone should be ashamed of having.

We will continue to look at more information about God the Father from the most astute and intelligent people that we can find.

Ante-Nicene Fathers, volume 2, contains writings of Clement of Alexandria, "The Stromata, or Miscellanies." Clement of Alexandria was a man who was not a Christian in his early life but conformed to the world around him. He, like so many individuals today, just went along for the ride, not making waves. When he became aware of the true meaning of life, he exploded with excitement and a thirst for the knowledge of the Lord. His accomplishments are much too great to list, but he was one of the greatest of all Christians in knowledge and works, which included his writing many books. Clement wrote the following three statements:

> God cannot be embraced in words or by the mind "For both is it a difficult task to discover the Father and Maker of this universe; and having found Him, it is impossible to declare Him to all. For this is by no means capable of expression, like the other subjects of instruction," says the truth loving Plato. (462)

> And when the Scripture says, "Moses entered the thick darkness where God was," this shows to those capable of understanding, that God is invisible and beyond expression by words. (463)

> To these statements the apostle will testify: "I know a man in Christ, caught up into the third heaven, and thence into Paradise, who heard unutterable words which it is not lawful for a man to speak,"—intimating thus the impossibility of expressing God, and indicating that what is divine is unutterable by human power. (463)

Theophilus of Antioch, another man who came out of the conformity of the world, was not only known as the earliest commentator of the

Gospels (as previously mentioned) but was known as the earliest historian of the Old Testament. In *Ante-Nicene Fathers*, volume 2, he wrote the following to Autolycus about God the Father:

> Though He be not visible to the eyes of the flesh, since He is incomprehensible. For if a man cannot look upon the sun, though it be a very small heavenly body, because of its exceeding heat and power, how shall not a mortal man be much more unable to face the glory of God, which is unutterable? (90)

Ante-Nicene Fathers, volume 4, contains the works of Origen De Principiis. Origen was simply brilliant; to say anything else would take away from his words. Origen wrote:

> Having refuted, them, as well as we could, every notion which might suggest that we were to think of God as in any degree corporeal, we go on to say that according to strict truth, God is incomprehensible, and incapable of being measured. (243)

> But among all intelligent, that is, incorporeal beings, what is so superior to all others—so unspeakably and incalculably superior—as God, whose nature cannot be grasped or seen by the power of any human understanding, even the purest and brightest? (243)

Ante-Nicene Fathers, volume 3, contains Tertullian's "A Treatise on the Soul." Tertullian, as I understand it, was the most prolific writer of all. We have over seven hundred pages of his work. Even today, it's hard to comprehend his intelligence and creative mind. After reading his books, I was in awe. Tertullian wrote, "Plato's Inconsistency. He Supposes the Soul Self-Existent, Yet Capable of Forgetting What Passed in a Previous State." He then adds, "The soul is immortal, incorruptible, incorporeal- since he believed God to be the same—invisible, incapable of delineation, uniform, supreme, rational, and intellectual" (203).

Volume 9 of *Ante-Nicene Fathers* contains "The Apology of

Aristides." Aristides was a philosopher who was able to take his works directly to the Roman emperor Hadrian. After listening to Aristides, Emperor Hadrian was inclined to write an *imperial rescript*, forbidding the punishment of Christians. Aristides wrote, "Whereas God is imperishable and unvarying, and invisible, while yet He sees, and overrules, and transforms all things" (266).

Volume 2 of *Ante-Nicene Fathers* contains Clemens Alexandrinus (Clement of Alexandria) on the "Salvation of the Rich Man." He wrote,

> For this is the immutable and immoveable source and support of life, the knowledge of God, who really is, and who bestows the things which really are, that is, those which are eternal, from whom both being and the continuance of it are derived to other beings. For ignorance of Him is death; but the knowledge and appropriation of Him, and love and likeness to Him, are the only life. (593)

Volume 2 of *Ante-Nicene Fathers* also contains Tatian's "Address to the Greeks." Tatian the Assyrian was a philosopher who deeply researched Greek philosophy and the religions of the Greeks. Thankfully, he became dismayed with all the speculations and all their gods and realized the truth of Christianity. Tatian wrote, "God alone is to be feared, —He who is not visible to human eyes, nor comes within the compass of human art" (66).

He also wrote,

> Our God did not begin to be in time: He alone is without beginning, and He Himself is the beginning of all things. God is a Spirit, not pervading matter, but the Maker of material spirits, and of the forms that are in matter; He is invisible, impalpable, being Himself the Father of both sensible and invisible things. Him we know from His creation and apprehend His invisible power by His works. (66)

At this point, I hope you understand how much information there is to support my comments on God the Father. God the Father is *beyond* beyond, but you do not have to accept my opinion for that. I have given a lot of information so far, and I will give you even more. It is critical to the understanding of God the Father. I will continue to quote the best sources that I know. I am inferior to these writers and am so glad that I have had the privilege and honor of reading their works.

In his book *The Universe Next Door*, James W. Sire writes,

> Of course God himself is forever so beyond us that we cannot have anything approaching total comprehension of him." (30)

In his book, *Christ the Center*, George A. F. Knight writes,

> No human mind, however brilliant, is able to classify and understand the mind of God any more than any ancient, Plato, Buddha or any other philosopher could ever do. (22)

Roger E. Olson and Christopher A. Hall, coauthors of *The Trinity*, write,

> How, in fact, can human beings adequately speak of God? The subject is too high. "For if you have been able to comprehend what you would say, it is not God; if you have been able to comprehend it, you have comprehended something else instead of God. If you have been able to comprehend Him as you think, by so thinking you have deceived yourself. (47–48)

> As Irenaeus criticizes gnostic cosmology, he is careful to describe his own theological methodology. In response to the Gnostics' inflated claims to knowledge of divine mysteries, Irenaeus advocates a much more restrained, sober course. He speaks of a "proper order

of … knowledge" and warns his readers not to "seek to rise above God himself." No one can fully understand the nature and purposes of God. To forget this will only lead to "trains of reflection opposed to your nature," with the final outcome a predictable foolishness." (26)

Second, the divine nature by definition "Cannot be named and is in effable. We say that every name, whether invented by human custom or handed down by the scriptures, is indicative of our conceptions of the divine nature, but does not signify what that nature is in itself," God's nature or essence remains "unlimited," "unnamable," "unspeakable," "in-comprehensible," and infinite." As "infinite," God's essence "is not limited in one respect while it is left unlimited in another, but infinity is free from limitation altogether. That therefore which is without limit is surely not limited by name." (38)

Carl Raschke writes in *The Next Reformation*, "We cannot positively state God's scale or character. We can only assert, that he is infinite, immutable, or unchanging" (57).

Alan Wolfe writes in *Transformation of American Religion,*

And in religion, whatever the Lord requires, knowledge of his teachings is not among them. 58 percent of Americans cannot name five of the Ten Commandments, just under half know that Genesis is the first book of the Bible, fewer than that can tell interviewers about the meaning of the Holy Trinity; and 10 percent of them believe that Joan of Arc was Noah wife. … This sociologist, a lesbian, went to Oregon to study the efforts by conservative Christian Churches to oppose a gay-rights referendum. She found conservative Christian activists' intent on doing just that, but she also found religious Christians "far less certain of themselves and their beliefs than I had anticipated, and the churches in which they placed their trust much more fractious." These are people who believe, often passionately, in God, even if they cannot tell others all that much about the God in which they believe. (72)

Part 2

God the Father Does Exist

CHAPTER 4

The Ontological Argument

YOU SHOULD BE CONVINCED BY now that no human being can communicate directly with God the Father in any way. Understanding this is the very beginning of a solid religious foundation. Understanding that no one can communicate directly with God the Father will release you from the mysticism surroundings religion. Religion, especially the Christian faith, is not a religion immersed in mysticism. The Christian faith is based on Jewish history and propositional truths in the scriptures. The Christian faith is based on logical and reasonable arguments, such as Anselm's ontological argument, Aquinas's cosmological argument, and the teleological argument. Anselm's ontological argument and the other two will be explained by using the book, *I Believe Because* by Batsell Barrett Baxter, PhD.

Concerning the ontological argument, Baxter writes,

> Anselm's Ontological Proof, In the late middle ages Anselm introduced to the philosophical and religious worlds a clever philosophical argument for the existence of God. While it is difficult both to understand and to appreciate, it deserves, to be stated and considered. It is, generally referred to as the ontological argument since ontology is that branch of philosophy that deals with the nature of being or existence. Anselm began with a definition, *"God is that than which nothing greater can be conceived!"* Then he argued that man is able to

conceive in his mind of the *idea* that than which there is no greater. At this point he introduced the statement, "But I can think of something that is greater than the *idea* of that than which there is no greater." Someone asked, "What?" The answer came: "The *existence* of that than which there is no greater." Hence, by very definition, God must exist. Turn this over in your mind. Does it have validity? Is it a mere conundrum? It is certainly difficult to disprove, yet there is a haunting feeling that it does not say much. Actually, if one grants Anselm's definition, then the argument seems to have validity. However, at best it is a philosophical argument much better suited to another age than our scientific twentieth century.

We are all familiar with the statement in the Psalms, "The fool hath said in his heart, There is no God." (Ps. 14:1). In order for the fool to say "God," he had to have a concept of God in his mind. To start out to deny God is a kind of implication that God exists. This, too, is a part of the ontological approach. Is it possible to think of something that does not exist? The reader is likely to think that it is easily possible to think of something that does not actually exist, but this is too quick a response. What we are really asking is, "Can you think of something that has never been thought of before, not just some new combination of previously known elements, but something that is absolutely new?" (41–42)

CHAPTER 5

The Cosmological Argument

IN REFERENCE TO THE COSMOLOGICAL argument, Batsell Barrett Baxter writes in *I Believe Because*,

> Credit has generally been given to Thomas Aquinas, who lived in the late Middle Ages, as the one who gave the world the classical statement of the cosmological argument for the existence of God. This is a set of arguments based on one central idea: the existing cosmos is an undeniable evidence of a creator. The argument is, based upon the general universal observation that "Nothing comes from nothing." Everything must have some antecedent cause. Hence, reasoning from the world, which obviously exists back to its creative cause, we find evidence that there must be some kind of creator. Aquinas stated his arguments in the following terms: *Unmoved mover-prime mover.* Unless there is an "infinite regress," there must be a first mover. We human beings experience movement, but we know that there is no perpetual motion. There must be some force, which started all movement. Therefore, there must be an unmoved mover or prime mover who started the universe. Thus, it is reasoned, God is the source behind the universe. *Uncaused first cause.* Everything is an effect of some cause. There is no effect which did not

have some antecedent cause behind it. Therefore, since there cannot be an "infinite regress," there must be an uncaused first cause. *Necessary being.* Everything in existence today is also capable of not existing. All natural things are *contingent,* that is, they are capable of being or not being. In an eternal time, every contingent thing would cease Then, there would be no world, but since there is there must be some force behind it—God.

There is a story which dates back to the time when the statesman Benjamin Franklin was Ambassador of, the United States to France. While living in Paris Franklin was a member of an elite literary social and scientific club. At certain meetings of this intellectual group, atheistic sentiments were expressed, leaving the impression that only the superstitious and uninformed still believed in God as the creator of the universe. At the next meeting of the group Benjamin Franklin brought a beautifully designed and executed model of the sun and our entire solar system. The earth and other planets were in their proper relationship to the sun and to each other and of appropriate sizes. It was a masterpiece. Upon seeing it, one of the sophisticated members of the club asked, "Who made it?" Dryly, without the trace of a smile, Franklin responded, "No one. It just happened." (53–54)

Dr. Baxter's conclusion is this:

Dr. Merritt Stanley Congdon, a natural scientist, puts the matter very simply but very well: "Many years ago I saw a beautiful, cultivated rosebush in bloom beside a lonely road in Pennsylvania. ... I *knew* intuitively that some mature human being had carefully planted it near his home." As each of the men quoted in this chapter, and countless others who might have been quoted, point out, the obvious existence of our universe is a powerful evidence that there must have been a creative force that brought it into existence. The atheist's position that the universe just happened, with no creator behind it, is a position difficult to uphold in the face of all the evidence around us. Without exception, we find that "Nothing comes from nothing." Are we to believeth, that the universe in its entirety is an exception to this universal law? Whatever force it is that brought our universe into being, we call God. (57)

CHAPTER 6

The Teleological Argument

NOW WE WILL CONSIDER MY favorite argument, the teleological argument. In *I Believe Because*, Dr. Baxter writes,

> Just as Thomas Aquinas is credited with the classical statement of the cosmological argument he is similarly credited with the definitive statement of the teleological argument for the existence of God. He classified this argument under a two-fold heading:
>
> 1. *Argument from design.* The universe demonstrates order and design hence there must be a designer. The existence of order and system demands an orderer. Beauty, form, design, and purpose in nature all imply a creative mind, an intelligent architect. This idea of purpose in nature and in life processes is opposed to the view of mechanism. It suggests that the force that brought the universe into being is an intelligent, planning, thinking being. (53)

We can see design in everything around us—the earth, the sky, the stars, the sea, our bodies, our food. For example, take one kernel of corn, bury it, and up grows a cornstalk that produces about eight cobs with about two hundred kernels. Maybe that is simple-minded of me, but it sure is design as far as I am concerned.

God the Father does not directly communicate with you or anyone else, but we can, with logical and reasonable information, understand that he does exist. Remember—do not listen to people who say or imply that they have heard directly from God the Father or that they know God the Father personally.

This Sunday, I heard a preacher on television say that God told *him* something directly. This kind of preaching is harmful and misleading, and it's one reason why so many people won't listen to anyone about religion. Remember when I talked about Goddians? I said Goddians are people who say they believe in God but know little or nothing about God. They might understand and think a little deeper about what they are saying if they were aware that *Satan believes* in God and is terrified of him. Satan knows about God the Father, Jesus, and the Bible.

Based on the previous information I've presented, it should be clear that God the Father does not communicate with people directly. So how *does* God the Father communicate with us? He communicates through a *manifestation*.

Webster's New Collegiate Dictionary defines manifestation in this way: "To make evident or certain by showing or displaying" (699).

God the Father has always used manifestations to communicate with people. A manifestation can be many different things; it could be a voice, an image, a vision, an angel, a dream, or a man.

Part 3

A Brief Understanding of Our Lord and Our God Jesus

CHAPTER 7

He Has Always Existed

THIS BRINGS US TO THE beginning of understanding our Lord and God, Jesus the Christ. Jesus was in the beginning with God the Father. I will again quote the best and the brightest in this area:

Ante-Nicene Fathers, volume 1, contains the epistle of Mathetes to Diognetus. Mathetes is thought to be the author mainly because of the way he presented himself, which to many sounded quite a bit like the apostle Paul. He may have been the first *apologist*, which I understand to be one who explains the scriptures to those who are not well acquainted with them. He wrote, "This is He who was from the beginning … This is He who, being from everlasting, is to-day the Son" (29).

Ante-Nicene Fathers, volume 1, also contains the epistle of Ignatius to the Magnesians. Ignatius and Polycarp were both disciples of the apostle John. It is wonderful and remarkable to me that I have had the great opportunity to read and write about those who discussed the things about the Lord directly with an apostle.

Ignatius wrote, "Jesus Christ, who was with the Father before the beginning of time" (61). "But that you may rather attain to a full assurance in Christ, who was begotten by the Father before all ages" (63).

In *Ante-Nicene Fathers*, volume 1, "Dialogue of Justin, Philosopher and Martyr with Trypho a Jew," Justin Martyr wrote,

> "I shall give you another testimony, my friends," said I,
> "from the Scriptures, that God begat before all creatures
> a Beginning, [who was] a certain rational power

[proceeding] from Himself, who is called by the Holy Spirit, now the Glory of the Lord, now the Son, again Wisdom, again an Angel, then God, and then Lord and Logos, and on another occasion He calls Himself Captain, when He appeared in human form to Joshua the son of Nave (Nun)." (227)

Ante-Nicene Fathers, volume 1, contains Irenaeus's "Against Heresies." Irenaeus wrote, "For the Son, being present with His own handiwork from the beginning ..." (469).

Ante-Nicene Fathers, volume 2, contains Clement of Alexandria's "Exhortation to the Heathens." Clement wrote, "The manifestation of the Word that was in the beginning, and before the beginning" (173).

Ante-Nicene Fathers, volume 2, Clement of Alexandria wrote, "He signifies by the appellation of the Father, that the Son also existed always, without beginning" (574).

Ante-Nicene Fathers, volume 2, "The Stromata, or Miscellanies": "Wherefore the Word is called the Alpha and the Omega, of whom alone the end becomes beginning, and ends again at the original beginning without any break" (438).

In *Ante-Nicene Fathers*, volume 3, Tertullian wrote "Against Praxeas": "It is the Son, therefore, who has been from the beginning" (611).

In *Ante-Nicene Fathers*, volume 4, Origen wrote "Against Celsus": "And although the Word which was in the beginning with God" (499).

"And yet let those who make this charge understand that He whom we regard and believe to have been from the beginning" (480).

"Who being in the beginning with God, became flesh" (604).

Also in volume 4, Origen wrote "Against Aelsus": "The Word, who was in the beginning, was with God" (642).

Ante-Nicene Fathers, volume 5, contains "Appendix to the Works of Hippolytus." Hippolytus wrote ten books. He was of Roman descent and a disciple of Irenaeus, who was a disciple of Polycarp, who was taught by the apostle John. He wrote, "Thou art the ever-living One. Thou art without beginning" (253).

Ante-Nicene Fathers, volume 6, contains Gregory Thaumaturgus's "Fourth Homily." In the third century AD, Gregory lived about twenty-six years as a heathen within the Roman society. He studied Roman law and came into contact with Origen, and after an intense program of study, he became a Christian. He wrote, "Thou who wast in the beginning" (69).

Ante-Nicene Fathers, volume 7, contains Victorinus's "Commentary on the Apocalypse of the Blessed John."

Another early Christian writer wrote the following: "We say that the measure of God's temple is the command of God to confess the Father Almighty, and that His Son Christ was begotten by the Father before the beginning of the world" (354).

In *Jesus as God—The New Testament Use of Theos in Reference to Jesus*, Murray J. Harris writes,

> But whereas the verse of the Torah continues, "God created," John follows with "the Word [already] existed." In Genesis the creation of the world is contemporaneous with or marks "the beginning"; in John the existence of the Word is anterior to "the beginning." (54)

> John implies the eternal preexistence of the Word. He who existed "in the beginning" before creation was himself without a beginning and therefore uncreated. There was no time when he did not exist. John is hinting that all speculation about the origin of the Logos is pointless. (54)

> Jesus not only was already at the beginning of creation John 1:1. At the time when Thomas spoke, and John wrote. (126)

In *Early Christian Doctrines*, J. N. D. Kelly writes,

> The chief interest of his theology, however, is the prominence it gives to Christ's pre-existence. It was He who cooperated with God the Father at creation (the words, 'Let us make man in our image', were addressed to Him); and He conversed with Moses, and before the

incarnation received His mandate from the Father. He is Lord of the cosmos', and it is His glory that all things are in Him, and unto Him'. (92)

In *Genesis in Space and Time*, Francis A. Schaeffer writes,

Although Genesis begins, "In the beginning," that does not mean that there was not anything before that." (16)

Jesus says that God the Father loved him prior to the creation of all else. And in John 17:5 Jesus asks the Father to glorify him, Jesus himself, "with the glory which I had with thee before the world was. There is, therefore, something that reaches back into eternity, —back before the phrase "in the beginning." Christ existed, and he had glory with the Father. (17)

The phrase "in the beginning" is repeated in Hebrews 1:10, and, as in John 1:1-3, it emphasizes the fact that Christ was already there before creation and was active in creation. (23)

In *God in Three Persons*, Millard J. Erickson writes,

With respect to Christ, Clement assumes his preexistence, since he spoke through the Spirit in the Psalms, and is the means by which God has always ruled. He is the "way in which we find our Savior, even Jesus Christ, the High Priest of all our offerings." Clement understands the Holy Spirit in terms of his inspiring God's prophets in all ages, the Old Testament writers as well as himself. (38)

Probably the most significant part of his theology however, is his emphasis on the preexistence of Christ. Christ was present and cooperated with God the Father at creation. (39)

In reference to Jesus, Murray J. Harris writes in *Jesus as God—The New Testament Use of Theos,*

> Jesus is described as the perfect representation of God's glory and nature (1:3); he not only existed before he appeared on earth (10:5), before Melchizedek (7:3), before human history began (1:2), or before the universe was created (1:10), but he also existed and exists eternally. (225)

This information is as convincing as any information could possibly be. Many people do not know that Jesus has always existed. Most people believe that he began his existence at his birth. This belief is an example of a *presupposition*. That idea has been stuck in their minds for their entire lives. Unless people study and think, they will not understand the truth. This applies to all of us and especially to Goddians. Remember— Goddians are people who believe in God but know little or nothing about him.

There is fact, and there is fiction, and there is ignorance. Most Goddians are ignorant because they don't care to know the truth, or they are just too lazy to understand that the subject they are ignoring means eternal death.

We know Jesus existed before time began and before creation. He is eternal. Jesus was also always with God the Father. Jesus was always God's communicator in the Old Testament and in the New Testament. Jesus is the one who spoke to the patriarchs and the prophets most of the time. Allow me to quote again the people who lived when Jesus was alive and others who lived and communicated with the apostles and other great writers.

Let's start with this question: who was talking to Adam and Eve in the garden of Eden?

In *Ante-Nicene Fathers*, volume 1, "Dialogue of Justin, Philosopher and Martyr with Trypho a Jew," Justin Martyr wrote,

> These and other such sayings are recorded by the lawgiver, and by the prophets; and I suppose that I have

stated sufficiently, that wherever God says, 'God went up from Abraham,' or, 'The Lord spake to Moses,' and 'The Lord came down to behold the tower which the sons of men had built, or when 'God shut Noah into the ark,' *you must not imagine that the unbegotten God Himself came down or went up from any place.* For, the ineffable Father and Lord of all neither has come to any place, nor walks, nor sleeps, nor rises up, but remains in His own place, wherever that is, quick to behold and quick to hear, having neither eyes nor ears, but being of indescribable might; and He sees all things, and knows all things, and none of us escapes His observation; and He is not moved or confined to a spot in the whole world, for He existed before the world was made. How then, could He talk with any one, or be seen by any one, or appear on the smallest portion of the earth, when the people at Sinai were not able to look even on the glory of Him who was sent from Him; and Moses himself could not enter into the tabernacle which he had erected, when it was filled with the glory of God; and the priest could not endure to stand before the temple when Solomon conveyed the ark into the house in Jerusalem which he had built for it? Therefore neither Abraham, nor Isaac, nor Jacob, nor any other man, saw the Father and ineffable Lord of all, and also of Christ, but [saw] Him who was according to His will His Son, being God, and the Angel because He ministered to His will; whom also it pleased Him to be born man by the Virgin; who also was fire when He conversed with Moses from the bush. (263)

Again, who was talking to Adam and Eve in the garden of Eden? Before we answer that question, let's look at some more quotes.

Ante-Nicene Fathers, volume 1, contains the "First Apology of Justin Martyr," in which he wrote,

When Moses was ordered to go down into Egypt and lead out the people of the Israelite who were there, and while he was tending the flocks of his maternal uncle in the land of Arabia, *our Christ* conversed with him under the appearance of fire from a bush. (184)

And he received mighty power *from Christ*, who spoke to him in the appearance of fire. (184)

The Jews, accordingly, being throughout of opinion that it was the Father of the universe who spake to Moses, though He who spake to him was *indeed the Son of God, who is called both Angel and Apostle*, are justly charged, both by the Spirit of prophecy and by *Christ Himself*, with knowing neither the Father nor the Son. For they who affirm that the Son is the Father, are proved neither to have become acquainted with the Father, nor to know that the Father of the universe has a Son; who also, being the first-begotten Word of God. (184)

And of old He appeared in the shape of fire and in the likeness of an angel to Moses and to the other prophets. (184)

And that which was said out of the bush to Moses, "I am that I am, the God of Abraham, and the God of Isaac, and the God of Jacob, and the God of your fathers," this signified that they, even though dead, are yet in existence, and are men belonging to Christ Himself. (184)

Justin Martyr wrote in *Ante-Nicene Fathers*, volume 1, "Dialogue of Justin with Trypho, a Jew,"

Permit me, further, to show you from the book of Exodus how this same One, who is both Angel, and God, and Lord, and man, and who appeared in human form to Abraham and Isaac. (226)

Now assuredly, Trypho, I shall show that, in the vision of Moses, this same One alone who is called an Angel, and who is God, appeared to and communed with Moses. (227)

"I shall give you another testimony, my friends," said I, "from the Scriptures, that God begat before all creatures a Beginning, [who was] a certain rational power [proceeding] from Himself, who is called by the Holy Spirit, now the Glory of the Lord, now the Son, again Wisdom, again an Angel, then God, and then Lord and Logos; and on another occasion He calls Himself Captain." (227)

Moreover, in the book of Exodus we have also perceived that the name of God Himself which, He says, was not revealed to Abraham or to Jacob, was *Jesus,* and was declared mysteriously through Moses. Thus, it is written: "And the Lord spake to Moses, Say to this people, Behold, I send My angel before thy face, to keep thee in the way, to bring thee into the land which I have prepared for thee. Give heed to Him; *and obey Him*; do not disobey Him. For He will not draw back from you; for *My name is in Him*." (236)

Now understand that He who led your fathers into the land is called by this name *Jesus,* and first called Auses (Oshea). (236)

And Jacob, having poured oil on a stone in the same place, is testified to by the very God who appeared to him, that he had anointed a pillar to the God who appeared to him. And that the stone symbolically proclaimed Christ. (242)

For I have proved that it was Jesus, who appeared to and conversed with Moses, and Abraham, and all the other patriarchs without exception, ministering to the will of the Father. (255)

"But if you knew, Trypho," continued I, "who He is that is called at one time the Angel of great counsel, and a Man by Ezekiel, and like the Son of man by Daniel, and a Child by Isaiah, and Christ and God to be worshipped by David, and Christ and a Stone by many, and Wisdom by Solomon, and Joseph and Judah and a Star by Moses, and the East by Zechariah, and the Suffering One and Jacob and Israel by Isaiah again, and a Rod, and Flower, and Corner-Stone, and Son of God." (262)

Ante-Nicene Fathers, volume 1, contains Irenaeus's "Against Heresies." Irenaeus wrote,

"When the Son speaks to Moses, He says, 'I am come down to deliver this people.'" (419)

"And the Word of God Himself used to converse with the ante-Mosaic patriarchs, in accordance with His divinity and glory." (428)

"He is the God of the living; and His Word is He who also spake to Moses." (467)

"Christ Himself, therefore, together with the Father, is the God of the living, who spake to Moses, and who was also manifested to the fathers." (467)

In *Ante-Nicene Fathers*, volume 2, Theophilus to Autolycus:

He, then, being Spirit of God, and governing principle, and wisdom, and power of the highest, came down upon the prophets, and through them spoke of the creation of the world and of all other things. For the prophets, were not when the world came into existence, but the wisdom of God, which was in Him, and His holy Word, which was always present with Him. Wherefore He speaks thus by the prophet Solomon. (98)

In *Ante-Nicene Fathers*, volume 2, Clement of Alexandria wrote "Exhortation to the Heathen":

And let us run to the Lord the Saviour, who now exhorts to salvation, as He has ever done, as He did by signs and wonders in Egypt and the desert, both by the bush and the cloud, which, through the favor of divine love, attended the Hebrews like a handmaid. (173)

He spake by the burning bush, for the men of that day needed signs and wonders. (173)

The Lord Himself speaking in *Isaiah, in Elias,* —speaking Himself by the mouth of the prophets. (173–174)

Daniel, so to induce them to reflect as to show them that He who remitted sins was God and man— that only Son of man, indeed, in the prophecy of Daniel, who had obtained the power of judging, and thereby, of course, of forgiving sins likewise (for He who judges also absolves); so that, when once that objection of theirs was shattered to pieces by their recollection of Scripture. (359)

Also in volume 2, Clement wrote "The Instructor":

Again, when He speaks in His own person, He confesses Himself to be the Instructor: "I am the Lord thy God, who brought thee out of the land of Egypt." Who, then, has the power of leading in and out? Is it not the Instructor? This was He who appeared to Abraham, and said to him, "I am thy God, be accepted before Me." (223)

Now that the Word was at once Jacob's trainer and the Instructor of humanity [appears from this]— "He asked," it is said, "His name, and said to him, tell me what Thy name is." And he said, "Why is it that thou askest My name?" For He reserved the new name for the new people—the babe; and was yet unnamed, the Lord God not having yet become man. Yet Jacob called the name of the place, "Face of God." "For I have seen," he says, "God face to face; and my life is preserved. "The face of God is the Word by whom God is manifested and made known." (224)

"It is He also who teaches Moses to act as instructor." (224)

Volume 2 of *Ante-Nicene Fathers* also contains "Fragments of Clemens Alexandrinus on the First Epistle of Peter." Clement wrote,

[Peter says] "Of which salvation," he says, "the prophets have inquired and searched diligently," and what follows. It is declared by this that the prophets, spake with wisdom, and that the Spirit of Christ was in them, according to the possession of Christ, and in subjection to Christ. For God works through archangels and kindred angels, who are called spirits of Christ. (571)

In *Ante-Nicene Fathers*, volume 3, The Writings of Tertullian, "The Prescription against Heretics," Tertullian wrote,

The law and the prophets, which preach Christ; as also in another place He says plainly, "Search the Scriptures, in which ye expect (to find) salvation; for they testify of me." (247)

That this Word is called His Son, and, under the name of God, was seen "in diverse manners" by the patriarchs, heard at all times in the prophets, at last brought down by the Spirit and Power of the Father. (249)

Tertullian wrote in "Against Marcion":

> Now we believe that Christ did ever act in the name of God the Father; that He actually from the beginning held intercourse with (men); actually, *communed with patriarchs and prophets*; was the Son of the Creator; was His Word; whom God made His Son by emitting Him from His own self. (318)

> It was *He* who was seen by the king of Babylon in the furnace with His martyrs: "the fourth, who was like the Son of man." *He* also was revealed to Daniel himself expressly as "the Son of man, coming in the clouds of heaven" as a Judge, as also the Scripture shows. (359)

> Now, that the very Lord Himself of all might, the Word and Spirit of the Father, was operating and preaching on earth.(374)

> This Christ also showed, when, recalling to notice (and no obliterating) those ancient wonders which were really His own. (393)

In "Against Praxeas VII," Tertullian wrote,

> But that He, was visible before the days of His flesh, in the way that He says to Aaron and Miriam, "And if there shall be a prophet amongst you, I will make myself known to him in a vision, and will speak to him in a dream; not as with Moses, *with whom I shall speak mouth to mouth,* even apparently, that is to say, in truth, and not enigmatically," that is to say, in image. (609)

> "Since, therefore, He reserves to some future time His presence and speech face to face with Moses—a promise which was afterwards fulfilled in the retirement of the

mount (of transfiguration), when as we read in the Gospel, *"Moses appeared talking with Jesus."* (609)

It is evident that in early times it was always in a glass, (as it were,) and an enigma, in vision and dream, that God, *I mean the Son of God, appeared—to the prophets and the patriarchs, as also to Moses indeed himself.* (609)

It is *the Son*, therefore, who has been *from the beginning administering* judgment, throwing down the haughty tower, and dividing the tongues, punishing the whole world by the violence of waters, raining upon Sodom and Gomorrah fire and brimstone, as the LORD from the LORD. For He was who at all times came down to hold converse with men, *from Adam on to the patriarchs and the prophets,* in vision, in dream, in mirror, in dark saying; ever from the beginning laying the foundation of the course of His dispensations, which He meant to follow out to the very last. (611)

"Ye have neither heard His voice at any time nor seen His shape;" thus affirming that in former times it was not the Father, but the Son, who used to be seen and heard. (616)

"Not that any man hath seen the Father;" thus showing us that it was through the Word of the Father that men were instructed and taught. (616)

In *Ante-Nicene Fathers*, volume 4, Origen De Principiis wrote in the preface,

And by the words of Christ we do not mean those only which He spake when He became man and tabernacled in the flesh; for before that time, Christ, the Word of God, was in Moses and the prophets. For without the

Word of God, how could they have been able to prophesy
of Christ? (239)

Ante-Nicene Fathers, volume 5, "The Extant Works and Fragments
of Hippolytus, Part II," contains the following (in writing of prophets
speaking of the prophets): "For these fathers were furnished with the
Spirit, and largely honored by the Word Himself; and just as it is with
instruments of music, so had they the Word always, like the plectrum,
in union with them, and when moved by Him the prophets announced
what God willed" (204).

In *Ante-Nicene Fathers*, volume 9, Origen's "Commentary on the
Gospel of John, Book I," he wrote,

> We must not, however, forget that the sojourning of
> Christ with men took place before His bodily sojourn, in
> an intellectual fashion, to those who were more perfect
> and not children, and were not under pedagogues
> and governors. In their minds they saw the fullness
> of the time to be at hand—the patriarchs, and Moses
> the servant, and the prophets who beheld the glory of
> Christ. (301)

> "How the Prophets and Holy Men of the Old Testament
> Knew the Things of Christ." (350)

In *Early Christian Doctrines*, J. N. D. Kelly writes, "That it was by
His word that He revealed Himself to the prophets" (10). Also:

> Further, when the Old Testament describes the
> appearance of the angel of Yahweh to the patriarchs,
> Philo's explanation is that in fact it was the Logos. (11)

> The second point is this: The Word of God, Son of
> God, Christ Jesus our Lord, Who was manifested to the
> prophets according to the form of their prophesying and
> according to the method of the Father's dispensation. (89)

He conversed with Moses, and before the incarnation received His mandate from the Father. (92)

So, in the Old Testament theophanies (here he was in full agreement with Justin) it was really the Word Who spoke with the patriarchs. (107)

As for the Spirit, it was He "through Whom the prophets prophesied." (107)

In *God in Three Persons*, Millard J. Erickson writes,

So, Irenaeus, writes, "The Son reveals the knowledge of the Father through His own manifestation, for the Son's manifestation is the making known of the Father." And the Son and Spirit are both involved in the inspiration of the prophets. (51)

In *New Testament Introduction* by Donald Guthrie, BD, MTh, PhD, he writes, "The prophet Isaiah is said to have seen the glory of Christ (xii. 41). The same prophet predicted the forerunner, a fact mentioned in all the Gospels" (238).

CHAPTER 8

He Created the Heavens and the Earth and Us

WE NOW KNOW THAT JESUS has always existed. We also know Jesus is the communicator of God the Father and always has been. This information, hopefully, has changed presuppositions or preconceived ideas in your mind about the preexistence and operations of Jesus before his birth on earth. Get ready for another change, as we are about to investigate the creation of the universe.

You may be able to recite the first sentence of the Bible: "In the beginning God created the heavens and the earth."

The apostle John wrote,

> In the beginning was the Word, and the Word was with God, and the Word was God. He was in the beginning with God; *all, things were made through him and without him was not anything made that was made.* In him was life, and the life was the light of man. (John 1:1–4, emphasis added)

Is there a contradiction here? No, God commanded, "Let there be light," and Jesus carried out God's will and made the light. This is not my opinion; it is a fact. The following quotes will verify my statements:

In *Ante-Nicene Fathers*, volume 1, "The Epistle of Mathetes to Diognetus," Mathetes wrote,

For, as I said, this was no mere earthly invention which was delivered to them, nor is it a mere human system of opinion, which judge it right to preserve so carefully, nor has a dispensation of mere human mysteries been committed to them, but truly God Himself, who is, almighty, the Creator of all things, and invisible, has sent from heaven, and placed among men, [*Him who is*] *the truth*, and the holy and incomprehensible Word, and has firmly established Him in their hearts. He did not, as one might have imagined, send to men any servant, or angel, or ruler, or any one of those who bear sway over earthly things, or one of those to whom the government of things in the heavens has been entrusted, *but the very Creator and Fashioner of all things*—by whom made He the heavens by whom he enclosed the sea within its proper bounds whose ordinances all the stars faithfully observe—from whom the sun has received the measure of his daily course to be observed — whom the moon obeys, being commanded to shine in the night, and whom the stars also obey, following the moon in her course; by whom all things have been arranged, and placed within their proper limits, and to whom all are subject—the heavens and the things that are therein, the earth and the things that are therein, the sea and the things that are therein—fire, air, and the abyss—the things which are in the heights, the things which are in the depths, and the things which lie between. (27)

In "The Epistle of Ignatius to the Ephesians," Ignatius wrote,

For the Son of God, who was begotten before time began, and established all things according to the will of the Father. (57)

When He made the foundations of the earth, I was with Him arranging. (228)

In *Ante-Nicene Fathers*, volume 1, "Dialogue of Justin with Trypho, a Jew," Justin Martyr wrote, "Just as Eve was made from one of Adam's ribs, and as all living beings were *created* in the beginning by the word of God" (241).

In *Ante-Nicene Fathers*, volume 1, Irenaeus wrote "Against Heresies":

> The disciple of the Lord therefore desiring to put an end to all such doctrines, and to establish the rule of truth in the Church, that there is one Almighty God, who made all things by His Word, both visible and invisible; showing at the same time, that *by the Word, through whom God made the creation,* He also bestowed salvation on the men included in the creation; thus commenced His teaching in the Gospel: "In the beginning was the Word, and the Word was with God, and the WORD was God. The same was in the beginning with God. *All things were made by Him, and without Him was nothing made.*" (226)

> The fallacy, then, of this exposition is manifest. For when John, proclaiming one God, the Almighty, and one Jesus Christ, the Only-begotten, *by whom all things were made,* declares that this was the Son of God, this the Only-begotten, this the Former of all things, this the true Light who enlighteneth every man, *this the Creator of the world,* this He that came to His own, this He that became flesh and dwelt among us. (329)

> The world was not formed by angels, or by any other being, contrary to the will of the most high God, but was made by the Father *through the Word.* (361)

> But it will not be regarded as at all probable by those who know that God stands in need of nothing, and that He created and *made all things by His Word.* (361)

"All things were made by Him, and without Him was nothing made." Now, among the "all things" our world must be embraced. It too, therefore, was made by His Word, as Scripture tells us in the book of Genesis *that He made all things* connected with our world by His Word. David also expresses the same truth [when he says] *"For He spake, and they were made; He commanded, and they were created."* (361–362)

For that all things, whether Angels, or Archangels, or Thrones, or Dominions, were both established and *created by Him who is God over all, through His Word,* John has thus pointed out. For when he had spoken of the Word of God as having been in the Father, he added, *"All things were made by Him, and without Him was not anything made.* David also, when he had enumerated [His] praises, subjoins by name all things whatsoever I have mentioned, both the heavens and all the powers therein: "For He commanded, and they were created; He spake, and they were made." Whom, therefore, did He command? The Word, no doubt, "by whom" he says, *"the heavens were established, and all their power by the breath of His mouth."* But that He did Himself make all things freely, and as He pleased. (421–422)

Answer to an objection, arising from the words of Christ (Matt. vi. 24). God alone is to be really called God and Lord, for He is without beginning and end. But one of created and subject things, shall ever be compared to the Word of God, *by whom all things were made,* who is our Lord Jesus Christ." (421)

One and the same God, the Creator of heaven and earth, is He whom the prophets foretold, and who was declared by the Gospel, proof of this, at the outset from St. Matthew's Gospel. (422)

John, however, does himself put this matter beyond all controversy on our part, when he says, *"He was in this world, and the world was made by Him."* (426)

And was formed by the hand of God, that is, *by the Word of God, for "all things were made by Him."* (454)

Because *the Word, the Maker of all things*, had formed beforehand for Himself the future dispensation of the human race. (454)

The *Lord the Maker of the world*; and by means of the formation [of man] the Artificer *who formed him.* (469)

Now, that the Word of God forms us in the womb, He says to Jeremiah, "Before I formed thee in the womb." (543)

For the Creator of the world is truly the Word of God: and this is our Lord, who in the last times was made man, existing in this world, and who in an invisible manner contains all things created. (546)

Ante-Nicene Fathers, volume 1, contains "Fragments from the Lost Writings of Irenæus":

With regard to Christ, the law and the prophets and the evangelists have proclaimed that He was born of a virgin, that He suffered upon a beam of wood, and that He appeared from the dead; that He also ascended to the heavens, and was glorified by the Father, and is the Eternal King; that He is the perfect Intelligence, the Word of God, who was begotten before the light; *that He was the Founder of the universe, along with it (light), and the Maker of man*; that He is All in all: Patriarch among the patriarchs; Law in the laws; Chief Priest among priests; Ruler among kings; the Prophet among prophets; the Angel among angels; the Man among men; Son in the Father; Son in the Father; God in God; King to all eternity. For it is He who sailed [in the ark] along with Noah, and who guided Abraham; who was bound along with Isaac, and was a Wanderer with Jacob; the Shepherd of those who are saved, and the Bridegroom of the Church; the Chief also of the cherubim, the Prince of the angelic powers; God of God; Son of the Father; Jesus Christ; King for ever and ever. Amen. (577)

In *Ante-Nicene Fathers*, volume 2, Theophilus to Autolycus, book I, Theophilus wrote,

Entrust yourself to the Physician, and He will couch the eyes of your soul and of your heart. Who is the Physician? God who heals and makes alive through His word and wisdom. *God by His own word and wisdom made all things*; for "by His word were the heavens made, and all the host of them by the breath of His mouth." Most excellent is His wisdom. *By His wisdom God founded the earth.* (91)

By Him He made all things. He is called "governing principle" [ἀρκή], because He rules, and is Lord of all things fashioned by Him." (98)

"It is God who made the heavens as a vault, and stretched them as a tent to dwell in." *The command, then, of God, that is, His Word,* shining as a lamp in an enclosed chamber, lit up all that was under heaven, when *He had made light* apart from the world." (100)

God, through His Word, next caused the waters to be collected into one collection, and the dry land to become visible, which formerly had been invisible. (100)

But to no one else than to His own Word and wisdom did He say, *"Let Us make."* (101)

But *His Word, through whom He made all things*, being His power and His wisdom, assuming the person of the Father and Lord of all, *went to the garden in the person of God, and conversed with Adam.* (103)

Ante-Nicene Fathers, volume 2, contains "A Plea for the Christians by Athenagoras the Athenian: Philosopher and Christian to the Emperors Marcus Aurelius Anoninus and Lucius Aurelius Commodus, Conquerors of Armenia and Sarmatia, and more than All Philosophers":

But that which is not *but has made all things by the Logos* which is from Him. (131)

That we are not atheists, therefore, seeing that we acknowledge one God, uncreated, eternal, invisible, impassible, incomprehensible, illimitable, who is apprehended by the understanding only and the reason, who is encompassed by light, and beauty, and spirit, and power ineffable, *by whom the universe has been created through His Logos, and set in order, and is kept in being.* (133)

But the *Son of God is the Logos* of the Father, in idea and in operation; for after the pattern of Him and *by Him were all things made.* (133)

In *Ante-Nicene Fathers*, volume 2, Clement of Alexandria wrote "Exhortation to the Heathen":

For the Word, who "was with God," and by whom all things were created, has appeared as our Teacher. The Word, who in the beginning bestowed on us life as Creator when He formed us. (173)

In "The Instructor," Clement wrote,

> "All Wisdom is from the Lord, and with Him for
> evermore;"—with authority of utterance, *for He is God
> and Creator: "For all things were made by Him, and
> without Him was not anything made."* (234)

> The view I take is, that *He Himself formed man* of the
> dust, and regenerated him by water; and made him grow
> by his Spirit. (234)

Clement of Alexandria wrote in "The Stromata or Miscellanies,"

> By faith we understand that *the worlds were framed by
> the word of God.* (349–350)

> But the nature of the Son, which is nearest to Him who
> is alone the Almighty One, is the most perfect, and most
> holy, and most potent, and most princely, and most kingly,
> and most beneficent. This is the highest excellence, which
> orders all things in accordance with the Father's will
> and holds the helm of the universe in the best way, with
> unwearied and tireless power, working all things in which
> it operates, keeping in view its hidden designs. (524)

In *Ante-Nicene Fathers*, volume 3, Tertullian wrote "The Prescription
against Heretics":

> You must know, that which prescribes the belief that
> there is one only God, and that He is none other than
> the Creator of the world, who *produced all things out of
> nothing through His own Word.* (242)

In "Against Marcion," Tertullian wrote,

> "All things," He says, "are delivered unto me of my
> Father." You may believe Him, if He is the Christ of the

Creator to whom all things belong; because the Creator has not delivered to a Son who is less than Himself all things, *which He created by Him, that is to say, by His Word.*" (390)

Since, then, He is the Son of man, I hold Him to be the Judge, and in the Judge I claim *the Creator.* (398)

"The Five Books against Marcion":

It follows that the apostle, when treating of the Creator, (as Him whom both Jew and Gentile as yet have) not known, means undoubtedly to teach us, that the *God who is to become known (in Christ) is the Creator.* (439)

As that "*Word of God by whom all things were made,* and without whom nothing was made." (470)

"Against Hermogenes":

"The Lord possessed me, the beginning of His ways *for the creation* of His works." For since *all things were made by the Wisdom of God,* it follows that, when God made both the heaven and the earth in principio — that is to say, in the beginning—*He made them in His Wisdom.* (488)

Tertullian in "Against Praxes":

"*By the Word of the Lord were the heavens made,* and all the hosts of them by His Spirit." Now this Word, the Power of God and the Wisdom of God, must be the *very Son of God.* (614)

Because *by the Word* were the *heavens established.* (615)

In *Ante-Nicene Fathers*, volume 4, Origen De Principiis's book I, Origen wrote, "For by Him were all things made" (240).

> Let him who is inclined to entertain this suspicion hear the undoubted declaration of Scripture pronouncing, "In wisdom hast Thou made them all," and the teaching of the Gospel, that "by Him were all things made, and without Him nothing was made." (250)

In *Ante-Nicene Fathers*, volume 4, Origen wrote "Against Celsus," Book II:

> For we assert that it was *to Him the Father gave the command*, when in the Mosaic account of the creation He uttered the words, *"Let there be light."* and *"Let there be a firmament,"* and gave the injunctions with regard to those other creative acts which were performed; and that to Him also were addressed the words, *"Let Us make man in Our own image* and likeness;" and that the *Logos, when commanded, obeyed* all the Father's will. And we make these statements not from our own conjectures, but because we believe the prophecies circulated among the Jews, in which it is said of God, and of the works of creation, in express words, as follows: *"He spake, and they were made; He commanded, and they were created."* (433)

> And that God *gave commandment* respecting the creation of such mighty things in the world, and they *were created*; and that He who received the command was God the *Logos*. (444)

> "He said, and it was done; *He commanded*, and all things stood fast;" remarking that the *immediate, Creator*, and, as it were, *very Maker of the world was the Word*, the Son of God; while the Father of the Word, by

commanding His own Son—the Word—to create the world, is primarily Creator. (601)

In seeing the image of the invisible God, we see *"the Creator and Father of the universe."* (628)

In *Ante-Nicene Fathers*, volume 5, "The Extant Works and Fragments of Hippolytus," Hippolytus wrote,

Even as the blessed John says, "For he sums up the things that were said by the prophets, and shows that this is the Word, by whom all things were made." (227)

The fact that *Christ, the Maker of all,* came down as the rain, and was known as a spring and diffused Himself as a river, and was baptized in the Jordan. (235)

We have seen the *Creator of all things* in the "form of a servant." (235)

In *Ante-Nicene Fathers*, volume 5, in the "Appendix to the Works of Hippolytus":

Thou art the ever-living One. Thou art without beginning, like the Father, and co-eternal with the Spirit. Thou art *He who made all things* out of nothing. (253)

Thou art He who *made us* (253), that the Trinity is equal perfectly in honour, and equal in glory, and has neither beginning nor end. *The Word is the Son of God, and is Himself the Creator of every creature, of things visible and invisible.* (257)

In *Ante-Nicene Fathers*, volume 5, Fathers of the Third Century, Hippolytus, Cyprian, Philip Schaff Caius, Novatian, Appendix—The

Treatises of Cyprian, we find, "He is the Wisdom of God, *by whom all things were made*" (515).

Novatian wrote in "Treaties Concerning the Trinity,"

> He commanded, and all things went forth: of whom it is written, "Thou hast made all things in wisdom." (613)

> But lest, from the fact of asserting that our Lord Jesus Christ, the Son of God, the Creator, was manifested in the substance of the true body. (620)

> For "by Him were made all the works, and without Him was nothing made." (622)

> For the world was made by Him. (622)

> It is most manifestly proved to be God. And, nevertheless, while the world itself is said to have been founded after Him, it is found to *have been created by Him;* by that very divinity in Him where by the world was made, both His glory and His authority are proved. (622)

> For since it is evident that *all things* were *made by Christ.* (623)

> It is written that *all things* were *made by Him.* (623)

> He is not man only, *but God* also, since all things are by Him. (623)

> That divine substance whose name is the Word, whereby *all things were made, and without whom nothing was made.* For all things are after Him, because they are by Him. And reasonably, He is before all things, but after the Father, since all things were made by Him, and

He proceeded from Him of whose will all things were made. Assuredly God proceeding from God. (643)

Ante-Nicene Fathers, volume 6, contains Gregory Thaumaturgus's "The Oration and Panegyric Addressed to Origen":

His first-born *Word, the Maker and Ruler of all things*, with whom also alone it is possible, both for Himself and for all, whether privately and individually, or publicly and collectively, to send up to the Father uninterrupted and ceaseless thanksgivings. (24)

This *Word created heaven and earth*, and in Him were all things made. (49)

She wrapped in swaddling-clothes Him who made every creature. (60)

He found no place, who by His word established heaven and earth. (60)

For in thy arms *the Creator of all things* shall be carried. (61)

In *Ante-Nicene Fathers*, volume 7, Lactantius wrote "The Divine Institutes, Book II, Of the Origin of Error":

God, therefore, when He began the fabric of the world, *set over the whole work that first and greatest Son*, and used Him at the same time as a counselor and *artificer, in planning, arranging,* and accomplishing, since He is complete both in knowledge, and judgment, and power; concerning whom I now speak more sparingly, because in another place both His excellence, and His name, and His nature must be related by us. (53)

Hermes, in the book which is entitled *The Perfect Word*, made use of these words: *"The Lord and Creator of all things,* whom we have thought right to call God, since He made the second God visible and sensible. But I use the term sensible, not because He Himself perceives (for the question is not whether He Himself perceives), but because He leads 5 to perception and to intelligence. Since, therefore, He made Him first, and alone, and one only." (105)

The Eritrean Sibyl, in the beginning of her poem, which she commenced with the Supreme God proclaims the *Son of God as* the *leader and commander of all,* in these verses. (105)

The nourisher and *creator of all things,* who placed the sweet breath in all, and made God the leader of all. (105)

Who was not *only begotten* at first before the world, but who also arranged it by His wisdom and constructed it by His might. (105–106)

On account of these impieties of theirs He cast them off for ever; and so, He ceased to send to them prophets. But He commanded *His own Son,* the first-begotten, the *maker of all things,* His own counsellor, to *descend from heaven,* that He might transfer the sacred religion of God to the Gentiles. (109)

Ante-Nicene Fathers, volume 7, contains Victorinus's "On the Creation of the World":

But the author of the whole creation is Jesus. His name is the Word; for thus His Father says: "My heart hath emitted a good word." John the evangelist thus says: "In the beginning was the Word, and the Word was with God, and the Word was God. The same was in the beginning with God. *All things were made by Him, and without Him was nothing made* that was made." Therefore, first, was made the creation; secondly, man, the lord of the human race, as says the apostle. Therefore this Word, when it made light, is called Wisdom; when it made the sky, Understanding; when it made land and sea, Counsel; when it made sun and moon and other bright things, Power; when it calls forth land and sea, Knowledge; when it formed man, Piety; when it blesses and sanctifies man, it has the name of God's fear. (342)

"Grace unto you, and peace, from Him which is, and which was, and which is to come." *He is*, because He endures continually; *He was*, because with the Father He made all things, and has at this time taken a beginning from the Virgin; *He is to come*, because assuredly *He will come* to judgment. (344)

He was described by the law, He was God's hand, and the Word of the Father from God, Lord over all, and founder of the world. (354)

Ante-Nicene Fathers, volume 9, contains the Diatessaron of Tatian, "The Text of the Diatessaron":

In the beginning was the Word, and the Word was with God, and God is the Word. This *was* in the beginning with God. *Everything was by his hand, and without him not even one existing thing was made.* (43)

In Origen's "Commentary on the Book of John," he wrote,

Life then came in the Word. And on the one side the Word is no other than the Christ, the Word, He who was with the Father, by whom all things were made. (307)

"How the Word is the Maker of All Things, and Even the Holy Spirit Was Made Through Him." (328)

All things were made through Him. (328)

And the Apostle Paul says in the Epistle to the Hebrews: "At the end of the days *He spoke to us in His Son,* whom *He made the heir of all things,* 'through whom' also He made the ages," showing us that God made the ages through His Son, the "through whom" belonging, when the ages were being made, to the Only-begotten. (328)

In *Jesus as God, The New Testament Use of Theos in Reference to Jesus*, Murray J. Harris writes (using the book of Hebrews),

Jesus is described as the perfect representation of God's glory and nature (1:3); he not only existed before he appeared on earth (10:5), before Melchizedek (7:3), before human history began (1:2), or before the universe was created (1:10), but he also existed and exists eternally (7:16; 9:14; 13:8); like his Father he may be called "Lord"; he is creator (1:10), sustainer,(1:3), and heir (1:2) of the universe, that is, everything in time and space (1:2); he is "Son" and "the Son of God" the timeless of (1:3) pointing to a natural, not adoptive, sonship; he is worshiped by angels (1:6) and is the object of human faith (12:2); he is sovereign over the world to come (2:5); and passages referring to Yahweh in the OT are applied to him. (225)

In *Baker's Dictionary of Theology*, Everett F. Harrison writes, "He is the pre-existent creator and the perpetual sustainer of the universe, the great Head of creation" (417).

In *Christ the Center*, author George A. F. Knight writes,

John's Gospel, consequently, when it seeks to tell us who Jesus is begins at the same place as Genesis 1:1.

John 1:1-3 runs "in the beginning was the Word, and the Word was with God (in his 'heart'), and the Word was God." (Note, the Word is no 'thing', but is 'He', on the ground that God is the 'living' God of the Hebrew text of the Old Testament.) "He was in the beginning with God. *All things came into being through him ...* What has come into being in him was life (the life of the living God), and the life was the light of all people. (31)

Early Christian Doctrines author, J. N. D. Kelly, writes,

The chief interest of his theology, however, is the prominence it gives to Christ's pre-existence. It *was He who cooperated with God the Father at creation ...*
    A rather fuller account is given by Athenagoras— "And by Him, all things were made." (JOHN 1:1) (133)

Genesis in Space and Time author, Francis A. Schaeffer, writes,

All things were made [became] by him. (22)

That same idea is repeated, though not the phrase itself, in Colossians 1:16–17, because there we are told that *"by him were all things created."* (23)

But to us there is but one God, the Father, of whom are all things, and for whom we exist; and *one Lord Jesus Christ, by whom are all things,* and we exist by him. Paul sets forth a parallel between the Father creating and the Son creating. (23)

Worthy art thou, our Lord and our God, to receive the glory and the honor and the power: for thou didst *create all things,* and because of thy will they were, and were created. (23)

In *God in Three Persons*, Millard J. Erickson writes,

> For with Him were always present the *Word and Wisdom*, the Son and the Spirit, by whom and in whom, freely and spontaneously, *"He made all things."*(50)

> Irenaeus says, "that we "should know that *He who made and formed ... and nourishes us by means of the creation,* establishing all things by His Word, and binding them together by His Wisdom-this is He who is the only true God." (51)

Is the Holy Spirit for Me? author, Harvey Floyd, writes,

> According to Hebrews, further, Christ is addressed as God by the Father (1:8), is Creator (1: 10). (15–16)

In *Jesus as God—The New Testament Use of Theos in Reference to Jesus*, Murray J. Harris writes,

> Like his Father he may be called "Lord"; *he is creator* (1:10), *sustainer*, (1:3), and *heir* (1:2) *of the universe*, that is, everything in time and space. (1:2). (225)

In *Lord Jesus Christ*, Larry W. Hurtado writes,

> The one through whom everything was created whether earthly or heavenly, visible or invisible, including all ranks of spiritual powers ("whether thrones, or dominions, or ruler, or powers"). The claim in the first line of 1:16 that all things were created in Christ is reiterated in slightly varied form and extended at the end this verse, where Christ is also the one "through" (dia) whom and "for" (eis) every-thing was made. (508)

In *New Testament Introduction*, Donald Guthrie, BD, MTh, PhD, writes,

> The Epistle contains a high Christology. Christ is preeminent over all other creatures and over creation itself. In fact, *all things were not only created by Him but for Him.* He is seen at the center of the universe sovereign over all principalities and powers, over all agencies which might challenge His authority. (551)

St. Athanasius, "On the Incarnation, The Treatise," wrote,

> We will begin, then, with the creation of the world and with God its Maker, for the first fact that you must grasp is this: *the renewal of creation has been wrought by the self-same Word Who made it in the beginning.* (26)

> By faith we understand that the worlds were framed by the Word of God. (28)

> He made all things out of nothing through His Word, our Lord Jesus Christ. (28)

> He, the Mighty One, the Artificer of all, Him-self prepared this. (34)

> By the Word of the Lord were the heavens made, and all the host of them by the Breath of His mouth. (99)

In *The Evangelization of the Roman Empire*, E. Glenn Hinson writes,

> The author of The Dialogue between Athanasius and Zaccheus adduced evidence from Wisdom and Word passages: in Psalm 103:24 God "made all things in wisdom," in Psalm 32:6, "The heavens were established by the Word of God." (252)

The Glory of Christ author, Jim Elliff, writes,

> Worthy are you, our Lord and God, to receive glory and honor and power, for you created all things, and by your will they existed and were created. (Rev. 4:8–11) (79)

In *The Glory of Christ*, general editor John H. Armstrong writes,

> For *by him all things were created,* in heaven and on earth, visible and invisible, whether thrones or dominions or rulers or authorities—all things were created through him and for him. (Col. 1:16) (24)

The Glory of Christ author R. Albert Mohler Jr. writes,

> To begin with, the title looks back to creation, where both Genesis 1 and John 1 converge to tell us *that Jesus Christ was Himself the mediator of creation.* "All things came into being through Him, and apart from Him nothing came into being that has come into being" (John 1:1). (59)

In *The Trinity*, Roger E. Olson and Christopher A. Hall write,

> Finally, John writes that it is through the pre-existent logos that creation itself has taken place (John 1:3). (7)

> Barnabas presents Christ as pre-existent, describing him as the one "to whom God said at the foundation of the world, Let us make man according to our image and likeness" (The Epistle of Barnabas 5:5). In the same text, Barnabas pictures the Son as "the Lord of the whole world." (19)

Now, we know God the Father cannot be communicated with directly. We know Jesus has always existed. We know Jesus is the communicator of God the Father in the Old Testament and in the New

Testament. We now know Jesus created the heavens and the earth and everything else, including you and me and every other human being. The Goddians do not know any of these things because they can't be bothered to know or they elect not to know. I hope the presuppositions and the preconceived ideas we talked about have been replaced with information, instead of what you think, believe, or feel.

We must deal with many more presuppositions before you have the educational foundation to live your life in peace, contentment, and happiness. This may seem like an *overload* of information, but this information can mean the difference between eternal life and horrifying, continuous death. I pray that the information I give you will help you live a life dedicated to the right philosophy of life, the right worldview. Remember, the way a person thinks is the way a person will act. It's time to continue to build the educational foundation.

CHAPTER 9

He Is the Mystery Revealed
in the Old Testament

IN THE OLD TESTAMENT, THERE was a mystery and a great anticipation of a future event that would give the people the greatest prominence in the world. They wanted the prestige and glorification of being the greatest nation on the earth. The Old Testament did give this impression to those people. The mystery was not only for them but for the entire human population of the world. The mystery was and is the most magnificent epiphany that has ever happened in human history. The inhabitants of the world are most fortunately reaping the benefits of that mystery. The mystery is the birth of Jesus. Here is where we again see how a person's presuppositions and preconceived ideas can result in a total misunderstanding of the birth of Jesus.

In *Ante-Nicene Fathers,* volume 1, Irenaeus wrote "Against Heresies":

> This is the mystery which he says was made known to him by revelation, that He who suffered under Pontius Pilate, the same is Lord of all, and King, and God, and Judge, receiving power from Him who is the God of all, because He became "obedient unto death, even the death of the cross. (433)

> True knowledge, then, consists in the understanding of Christ, which Paul terms the wisdom of God hidden in a mystery. (574)

In *Ante-Nicene Fathers,* volume 2, Clement of Alexandria wrote "The Stromata, or Miscellanies" Book V:

> For the Word Himself is the manifest mystery: God in man, and man God. And the Mediator executes the Father's will; for the Mediator is the Word, who is common to both—the Son of God, the Savior of men. (27)

> In confirmation of these things, in the Epistle to the Corinthians the apostle plainly says: "Howbeit we speak wisdom among those who are perfect, but not the wisdom of this world, or of the princes of this world, that come to naught. But we speak the wisdom of God hidden in a mystery." And again, in another place he says: "To the acknowledgment of the mystery of God in Christ, in whom are hid all the treasures of wisdom and knowledge." (463)

Ante-Nicene Fathers, volume 4, contains Origen's "Against Celsus," Book I. Origen writes, "The mystery according to revelation, which was kept secret since the world began, but now is made manifest in the Scriptures of the prophets, and by the appearance of our Lord Jesus Christ" (43).

In *Ante-Nicene Fathers,* volume 6, Gregory Thaumaturgus wrote "The First Homily on the Annunciation to the Holy Virgin Mary":

> To-day is the whole circle of the earth filled with joy, since the sojourn of the Holy Spirit has been realized to men. To-day the grace of God and the hope of the unseen shine through all wonders transcending imagination and make the mystery that was kept hid from eternity plainly discernible to us. (58)

In *Ante-Nicene Fathers,* volume 7, Lactantius wrote "The Epitome of the Divine Institutes":

> It follows that no other hope is proposed to man, unless he shall follow true religion and true wisdom, which

is in Christ, and he who is ignorant of Him is always estranged from the truth and from God. Nor let the Jews, or philosophers, flatter them-selves respecting the Supreme God. He who has not acknowledged the Son has been unable to acknowledge the Father. This is wisdom, and this is the mystery of the Supreme God. God willed that He should be acknowledged and worshipped through Him. On this account He sent the prophets beforehand to announce His coming, that when the things which had been foretold were fulfilled in Him, then He might be believed by men to be both the Son of God and God. (242)

The Global God authors, Aida Besancon Spencer and William David Spencer, write, "The sacrifice of God in Christ stands at the center of this mystery." (41)

The most beneficial mystery in the history of humankind has been revealed. People are now honored and blessed to be a part of the appearance of Jesus, our Lord and our God.

Here is where a person's presuppositions and preconceived ideas can result in a total misunderstanding of the birth of Jesus. The word *birth* is often associated with a beginning of a new human life. We also may think of the natural process of human life, which is, a man and a woman together, creating a life. Although this is a natural and correct understanding of the birth of a human being, it does not apply to Jesus. Jesus did not have a beginning at his birth; Jesus has always been. Jesus also did not have a natural birth, as we understand natural birth. Jesus did not have a natural father or mother who together created him, although Mary was chosen to accommodate the birth of Jesus. Humans did not have any participation in the forming of Jesus but only the delivery process.

Jesus's birth was similar to Adam's creation, which was by spiritual means. This was the mystery promised long ago, which was that God would enter humanity as a human named Jesus.

Matthew 1:23 says, "Now all this took place that what was spoken by the Lord, through the prophet might be fulfilled, saying, Behold, the virgin shall be with child, and shall bear a son, and they shall call His name Immanuel, which translated means, God with us." This is God's coming to earth as a person, like one of us. This is not only the mystery; it is the greatest happening in human history. It happened as the Old Testament prophets predicted. As Moses said in Deuteronomy, "We shall see in that day that God will talk to man, and he shall live."

Luke 2:7 tells us, "And she gave birth to her first-born son; and she wrapped Him in cloths, and laid Him in a manger, because there was no room for them in the inn." A manger is an animals' feeding trough.

Now we know that God the Father cannot be communicated with directly. We know Jesus has always existed. We know Jesus is the communicator of God the Father in the Old Testament and in the New Testament. We now know Jesus created the heavens and the earth and everything else, including you and me and every other human being. We know the mystery, which was hidden for thousands of years, is the birth of Jesus here on earth. We also know the birth of Jesus was not a natural human birth but a spiritual process.

CHAPTER 10

He Is Misunderstood as Just the Son of God.

MANY OF US ARE FAMILIAR with the scripture of John 3:16, which says, "For God so loved the world, that He gave His only begotten Son, that whoever believes in Him should not perish, but have eternal life." The word *Son* in the scripture does not refer to a male child of a man and woman. As mentioned previously, Jesus was not conceived in the same manner as humans are conceived. Therefore, the word *son*—as we would refer to a male child who was born to a man and a woman—does not apply to him. We need to address Jesus as *Son*.

In his book *The Names of God*, George W. Knight lists 151 different names that refer to Jesus. They are as follows:

> advocate, alive for evermore, all, and in all, almighty, blessed and only potentate, branch of righteousness, bread, bridegroom, bright and morning star, brightness of god's glory, captain of salvation, captain of the host of the lord, carpenter, chief cornerstone child Jesus, chosen of god, Christ, Christ crucified, Christ Jesus our Lord, consolation of Israel, counselor, covenant of the people, Daysman, dayspring from on high, deliverer, desire of all nations, door, elect, end of the law, ensign for the nations, eternal life, everlasting Father, everlasting light, express image, faithful, faithful and true, faithful and true witness, faithful creator, first begotten, firstborn

from the dead, first fruits, flesh, foreordained before the foundation of the world, forerunner, foundation, fountain, friend of publicans and sinners, fullers' soap, gift of god, glory of Israel, God, good master, good shepherd, governor, greater than Jonas/greater than Solomon, great high priest, great prophet, head of all principality and power, head of the church, head of the corner, heir of all things, high priest after the order of Melchisedec, holy one/holy one of God, hope of glory, horn of salvation, I am, Immanuel/Emmanuel, Jesus, Jesus of Galilee/Jesus of Nazareth, Judge of the quick and dead, just king, king, king of kings, king of saints, king of the Jews, lamb, lamb of God, lamb slain from the foundation of the world, last Adam, leader and commander to the people, life, light, light of the world, lion of the tribe of Judah, living stone, Lord, Lord from heaven, Lord of Lords, Lord of peace, Lord of the dead and living, Lord of the harvest, Lord of the Sabbath, Lord over all, Lord's Christ, man of Gods right hand, man of sorrows, master, mediator, mediator of the new testament, messenger of the covenant, Messiah, Minister of the true tabernacle, one chosen out of the people, only begotten son, only wise God, our Passover, physician, plant of renown, power of God, Prince, Prince of Princes, Prince of the kings of the earth, propitiation for our sins, quickening Spirit, Rabbi / Rabboni, Redeemer, refiner's fire, resurrection and the life, righteous, righteous servant, rod out of the stem of Jesse, root and offspring of David, Saviour, Saviour of the body, Sceptre out of Israel, seed of the woman, Shiloh, son of Abraham, on of David, son of God, son of Joseph, son of man, son of Mary, son over his own house, spiritual rock, star out of Jacob, teacher come from God, truth, vine, way, word

I have listed them so that you understand that Jesus is referred to in many ways. The word *son* is not necessarily the most prominent term used for Jesus, and the word *Son* is not referred to as much as other titles. Jesus referred to himself as the son of man more than any other title. He does not refer to himself as Son of God.

In his book *Jesus as God*, Murray J. Harris provides an outline, which says, in part:

> 2. Divine titles claimed by or applied to Jesus, a. Son of man, b. Son of God, c. Messiah, d. Lord, e. Alpha and Omega, f. God. Therefore, Jesus should not, be compared to a son of a man and a woman. Harris also writes, "Applied to Jesus as the Son of God, it will mean that he is without spiritual Siblings and without equals. He is "sole-born" and "peerless." No one else can lay claim to the title Son of God in the sense in which it applies to Christ. (87)

He also writes that Jesus is

> "unique" (a) in relation to the Father, because (I) both before and after his incarnation he was in the most intimate fellowship with his Father. (1:18) (ii) He was the sole an matchless Revealer of the Father's love. (John 3:16; 1 John 4:9), And (iii) his origin is traceable to God the Father. (John 1:14; 73 cf. 1 John 5:18); and (b) in relation to human beings, because he is the object of human faith, the means of eternal salvation, and the touchstone of divine judgment (John 3:16,18). (87)

The idea of Jesus being a son, like a son born to a couple on earth, should not be compared to Jesus's Sonship to God the Father, although Jesus was totally human.

Now we know God the Father cannot be communicated with directly. We know Jesus has always existed. We know Jesus is the communicator of God the Father in the Old Testament and in the New Testament and that he created the heavens and the earth and everything else, including you and me and every other human being. We know the mystery hidden for thousands of years is the birth of Jesus here on earth and that the birth of Jesus was not a natural human birth but a spiritual process. We know that the idea of Jesus's being the Son of God the Father is not to be compared to what we normally think of as a son born to a natural mother and father. Jesus is not *a son* of God the Father; he is *the only Son* of God the Father.

All this information is to help you to understand the most misleading presupposition of all time. It is one that has caused more confusion and division among religious people than any other preconceived idea has every caused, and that is that people think they can rely on God the Father. According to all scripture, Jesus is our Lord and our God, and all things human must go through him. If we do not go to and through Jesus, there is no relationship with God the Father.

A chain of command has been set up by God the Father. Think of the military chain of command. When people join a branch of the military service, they are given a rank, such as private, and the ranking goes up to sergeant major of the army for noncommissioned officers. Next, there are the commissioned officers, which are second lieutenant, first lieutenant, captain, major, lieutenant colonel, full-bird colonel, brigadier general, major general, lieutenant general, general, chief of staff the army, joint chief of staff, the secretary of defense, and the president of the United States. When the private has a complaint or any other concern, he must first report his concerns to the next in command; he cannot go to any other person until he first reports to his next in command. That could be his squad leader, who could be a private first class. No matter what he thinks, no matter what he believes, no matter how he feels, he cannot address his concerns to anyone else until he follows the chain of command. That is a direct order he must follow, or he will receive disciplinary action.

Likewise, people must go through Jesus for all their concerns. Jesus is totally and exclusively the authority of our universe. No matter what we might believe, no matter what we think, and no matter what we might feel, Jesus is our God.

Now, I will give you all the information that I have gathered over the last forty-three years. I hope that you will understand that Jesus is the *foundation* on which you must build your spiritual education.

CHAPTER 11

He Is the Manifestation of God the Father Himself.

YOU ARE ABOUT TO READ information from many writers who lived in the first century to the fourth century. Some of them were with and were instructed by the apostles, such as Clement, mentioned by the apostle Paul in the book of Philippians 4:3. Clement is said to have been a friend of the apostle Paul and traveled with him on many occasions. Other writers quoted are well-known respected Christian writers.

In *Ante-Nicene Fathers*, volume 1, "The First Epistle of Clement to the Corinthians," Clement wrote,

> Content with the provision which God had made for you, and carefully attending to His words, ye were inwardly filled with His doctrine, and His sufferings were before your eyes. (5)

In *Ante-Nicene Fathers*, volume 1, "The Epistle of Mathetes to Diognetus," Mathetes wrote the following:

> For, as I said, this was no mere earthly invention which was delivered to them, nor is it a mere human system of opinion, which they judge it right to preserve so carefully, nor has a dispensation of mere human mysteries been committed to them, but truly God Himself, who is, almighty, the Creator of all things, and invisible, has sent

from heaven, and placed among men, [Him who is] the truth, and the holy and incomprehensible Word, and has firmly established Him in their hearts. He did not, as one might have imagined, send to men any servant, or angel, or ruler, or any one of those who bear sway over earthly things, or one of those to whom the government of things in the heavens has been entrusted, but the very Creator and Fashioner of all things—by whom made He the heavens by whom he enclosed the sea within its proper bounds whose ordinances all the stars faithfully observe—from whom the sun has received the measure of his daily course to be observed—whom the moon obeys, being commanded to shine in the night, and whom the stars also obey, following the moon in her course; by whom all things have been arranged, and placed within their proper limits, and to whom all are subject—the heavens and the things that are therein, the earth and the things that are therein, the sea and the things that are therein—fire, air, and the abyss—the things which are in the heights, the things which are in the depths, and the things which lie between. As a king sends his son, who is also a king, so sent He Him; as God. (27)

For, who of men at all understood before His coming what God is? Do you accept of the vain and silly doctrines of those who are deemed trustworthy philosophers? Of whom some said that fire was God, calling that God to which they themselves were by and by to come; and some water; and others some other of the elements formed by God. (28)

No man has either seen Him, or made Him known, but He has revealed Himself. And He has manifested Himself through faith, to which alone it is given to behold God. For God, the Lord and Fashioner of all things, who made all things.

But after He revealed and laid open, through His beloved Son, the things which had been prepared from the beginning. (28)

In *Ante-Nicene Fathers*, volume 1, "The Epistle of Polycarp to the Philippians," Polycarp wrote the following:

I have greatly rejoiced with you in our Lord Jesus Christ, because ye have followed the example of true love [as displayed by God], and have accompanied, as became you, those who were bound in chains, the fitting ornaments of saints, and which are indeed the diadems of the true elect of God and our Lord; and because the strong root of your faith, spoken of in days long gone by. (33)

I exhort you all, therefore, to yield obedience to the word of righteousness, and to exercise all patience, such as ye have seen [set] before your eyes, not only in the case of the blessed Ignatius, and Zosimus, and Rufus, but also in others among yourselves, and in Paul himself, and the rest of the apostles. (35)

But I have neither seen nor heard of any such thing among you, in the midst of whom the blessed PAUL labored. (35)

In *Ante-Nicene Fathers*, volume 1, "The Encyclical Epistle of the Church at Smyrna Concerning the Martyrdom of the Holy Polycarp, the Church at Smyrna wrote:

And he, placing his hands behind him, and being bound like a distinguished ram [taken] out of a great flock for sacrifice, and prepared to be an acceptable burnt-offering unto God, looked up to heaven, and said, "O Lord God Almighty, the Father of thy beloved and blessed Son Jesus Christ, by whom we have received the knowledge of Thee, the God of angels and powers, and of every creature, and of the whole race of the righteous who live before thee. (42)

Ante-Nicene Fathers, volume 1, contains "The Epistle of Ignatius to the Ephesians." Ignatius wrote,

We have also as a Physician the Lord our God, Jesus the Christ, the only-begotten Son and Word, before time began, but who afterwards became also man, of Mary the virgin. For the Word was made flesh. (52)

BUT THE HOLY Spirit does not speak His own things, but those of Christ, and that not from himself, but from the Lord; even as the Lord also announced to us the things that He received from the Father. For, says He, "the word which ye hear is not Mine, but the Father's, who sent Me." And says He of the Holy Spirit, "He shall not speak of Himself, but whatsoever things He shall hear from Me." And He says of Himself to the Father, "I have," says He, "glorified Thee upon the earth; I have finished the work which, Thou gavest Me; I have manifested Thy name to men." And of the Holy Ghost, "He shall glorify Me, for He receives of Mine." (53)

Our Lord and God, Jesus Christ, the Son of the living God, first did and then taught, as Luke testifies, "whose praise is in the Gospel through all the Churches. (56)

And the old kingdom abolished, God Himself being manifested in human form for the renewal of eternal life. (57)

In *Ante-Nicene Fathers*, volume 1, "The Epistle of Ignatius to the Magnesians," Ignatius also wrote,

I pray for a union both of the flesh and spirit of Jesus Christ, "who is the Saviour of all men, but specially of them that believe;" by whose blood ye were redeemed; by whom ye have known God, or rather have been known by Him. (59)

For the divinest prophets lived according to Jesus Christ. On this account also they were persecuted, being inspired by grace to fully convince the unbelieving that there is one God, the Almighty, who has manifested Himself by Jesus Christ His Son, who is His Word. (62)

He made known the one and only true God, His Father. (64)

In *Ante-Nicene Fathers*, volume 1, "The Epistle of Ignatius to the Trallians," Ignatius wrote,

Word was truly born of the Virgin, having clothed Himself with a body of like passions with our own. He who forms all men in the womb, was Himself really in the womb. (71)

And the Father, who always hears Him, answered and said, "Arise, O God, and judge the earth; for Thou shall receive all the heathen for Thine inheritance." (71)

God, who is [the Saviour] Himself. (71)

In "The Epistle of Ignatius to the Romans," he wrote,

The Church which is beloved and enlightened by the will of Him that willeth all things which are according to the love of Jesus Christ our God. (73)

The Church which is sanctified and enlightened by the will of God, who formed all things that are according to the faith and love of Jesus Christ, our God and Saviour. (71)

Nothing visible is eternal. "For the things which are seen are temporal, but the things which are not seen are eternal." For our God, Jesus Christ, now that He is with the Father, is more revealed [in His glory]. (74)

He is the mouth altogether free from falsehood, by which the Father has truly spoken. (77)

In "The Epistle of Ignatius to the Philadelphians," Ignatius wrote,

For there is one flesh of the Lord Jesus Christ; and His blood which was shed for us is one; one loaf also is broken to all [the communicants], and one cup is distributed among them all: there is but one altar for the whole Church, and one bishop, with the presbytery and deacons, my fellow servants. Since, also, there is but one unbegotten Being, God, even the Father; and one only begotten Son, God, the Word and man; and one Comforter, the Spirit of truth; and, one preaching, and one faith, and one baptism; and one Church which the holy apostles established. (81)

In "The Epistle of Ignatius to Polycarp," Ignatius continues to write the following:

Look for Christ, the Son of God; who was before time, yet appeared in time; who was invisible by nature, yet visible in the flesh; who was impalpable, and could not be touched, as being without a body, but for our sakes became such, might be touched and handled in the body; who was impassible as God, but became passable for our sakes as man; and who in every kind of way suffered for our sakes. (94)

I pray for your happiness forever in our God, Jesus Christ, by whom continue ye in the unity and under the protection of God. (96)

In *Ante-Nicene Fathers*, volume 1, "The First Apology of Justin," Justin Martyr wrote the following:

Wherefore, too, the angel said to the virgin, "Thou shalt call His name Jesus, for He shall save His people from their sins." And that the prophets are inspired by no other than the Divine Word, even you, as I fancy, will grant. (174)

But when you hear the utterances of the prophets spoken as it were personally, you must not suppose that they are spoken by the inspired themselves, but by the Divine Word who moves them. For sometimes He declares things that are to come to pass, in the manner of one who foretells the future; sometimes He speaks as from the person of God the Lord and Father of all; sometimes as from the person of Christ; sometimes as from the person of the people answering the Lord or His Father, just as you can see even in your own writers, one man being the writer of the whole, but introducing the persons who converse. And this, the Jews who possessed the books of the prophets did not understand, and therefore did not recognize Christ even when He came, but even hate us who say that He has come, and who prove that, as was predicted, He was crucified by them. (175)

And Jesus the Christ, because the Jews knew not what the Father was, and what the Son, in like manner accused them; and Himself said, "No one knoweth the Father, but the Son; nor the Son, but the Father, and they to whom the Son revealeth Him." Now the Word

of God is His Son, as we have before said. And He is
called Angel and Apostle; for He declares whatever we
ought to know and " ... is sent forth to declare whatever
is revealed; as our Lord Himself says, "He that heareth
Me, heareth Him that sent Me." From the writings of
Moses also this will be manifest; for thus it is written in
them, "And the Angel of God spake to Moses, in a flame
of fire out of the bush, and said, I am that I am, the God
of Abraham, the God of Isaac, the God of Jacob, the God
of thy fathers." (184)

And appearing sometimes in the form of fire, and
sometimes in the likeness of angels; but now, by the will
of God, having become man for the human race. (184)

In *Ante-Nicene Fathers*, volume 1, "Dialogue of Justin, Philosopher
and Martyr, with Trypho, a Jew," Justin Martyr also wrote the following:

And I said, "As you wish, Trypho, I shall come to these
proofs which you seek in the fitting place; but now you
will permit me first to recount the prophecies, which I
wish to do to prove that Christ is called both God and
Lord of hosts." (212)

God who appeared to Moses is distinguished from
God the Father. "Moses, then, the blessed and faithful
servant of God, declares that He who appeared to
Abraham under the oak in Mamre is God, sent with the
two angels in His company to judge Sodom by Another
who remains ever in the super celestial places, invisible
to all men, holding personal intercourse with none,
whom we believe to be Maker and Father of all things;
for he speaks thus: 'God appeared to him under the oak
in Mamre, as he sat at his tent-door at noontide. And
lifting his eyes, he saw, and behold, three men stood
before him; and when he saw them, he ran to meet them

from the door of his tent; and he bowed himself toward the ground, and said;' (and so on). (223)

But also [for what is said] by David. For there is written by him: 'The Lord says to my Lord, Sit on My right hand, until I make Thine enemies Thy footstool,' (Psa. 110:1) as I have already quoted. And again, in other words: 'Thy throne, O God, is for ever and ever. A sceptre of equity is the sceptre of Thy kingdom: Thou hast loved righteousness an hated iniquity: therefore God, even Thy God, hath anointed Thee with the oil of gladness above Thy fellows.' If therefore, you assert that the Holy Spirit calls some other one God and Lord, besides the Father of all things and His Christ, answer me; for I undertake to prove to you from Scriptures themselves, that He whom the Scripture calls Lord is not one of the two angels that went to Sodom, but He who was with them, and is called God, that appeared to Abraham. (224)

"The Lord rained down upon Sodom and Gomorrah Sulphur and fire from the Lord out of heaven." (225)

It is again written by Moses, my brethren, that He who is called God and appeared to the patriarchs is called both Angel and Lord, in order that from this you may understand Him to be minister to the Father of all things, as you have already admitted, and may remain firm, persuaded by additional arguments. The word of God, therefore, [recorded] by Moses, when referring to Jacob the grandson of Abraham, speaks thus. (225)

For I have seen what Laban doeth unto thee; I am the God who appeared to thee in Bethel. (225)

Thou hast prevailed with God. (226)

I saw God face to face. (226)

Bethel; for their God appeared to him when he fled from the face of his brother Esau. (226)

God appeared again to Jacob in Luz. (226)

And God said to him, Thy name shall be no more called Jacob, but Israel shall be thy name.' He is called God, and He is and shall be God. (226)

Permit me, further, to show you from the book of Exodus how this same One, who is both Angel, and God, and Lord, and man, and who appeared in human form to Abraham and Isaac. (226)

"Go and gather the elders of Israel, and thou shalt say unto them, The Lord God of your fathers, the God of Abraham, the God of Isaac, and the God of Jacob, hath appeared to me." (226)

Now assuredly, Trypho, I shall show that, in the vision of Moses, this same One alone who is called an Angel, and who is God, appeared to and communed with Moses. (227)

"I shall give you another testimony, my friends," said I, "from the Scriptures, that God begat before all creatures a Beginning, [who was] a certain rational power [proceeding] from Himself, who is called by the Holy Spirit, now the Glory of the Lord, now the Son, again Wisdom, again an Angel, then God, and then Lord and Logos; and on another occasion He calls Himself Captain," (227)

The Word of Wisdom, who is Himself this God begotten of the Father of all things, and Word, and Wisdom, and Power, and the Glory of the Begetter, will bear evidence to me, when He speaks by Solomon the following: 'If I shall declare to you what happens daily, I shall call to mind events from everlasting, and revived them. The Lord made me the beginning of His ways for His works. From everlasting He established me in the beginning, before He had made the earth, and before He had made the deeps, before the springs of the waters had issued forth, before the mountains had been established. Before all the hills He begets me. God made the country, and the desert, and the highest inhabited places under the sky. When He made ready the heavens, I was along with Him, and when He set up His throne on the winds: when He made the high clouds strong, … and the springs of the deep safe, when He made the foundations of the earth, I was with Him arranging. I was that in which He rejoiced; daily and at all times I delighted in His countenance, because He delighted in the finishing of the habitable world and delighted in the sons of men. (228)

And Joshua approached to Him, and said, Art thou for us, or for our adversaries? And He said to him, I am Captain of the Lord's host. (228)

"And Joshua fell on his face on the ground, and said to Him, Lord, what commandest Thou Thy servant?" (228)

It is proved that this God was incarnate. (228)

Therefore, these words testify explicitly that He is witnessed to by Him who established these things, as deserving to be worshipped, as God and as Christ. (229)

"Here Trypho, said "Let Him be recognized as Lord and Christ and God, as the Scriptures declare, by you of the Gentiles, who have from His name been all called Christians; but we who are servants of God that made this same [Christ], do not require to confess or worship Him." (229)

In order that you may recognize Him as God coming forth from above, and man living among men; and [how it is declared] that He will again appear. (230)

And Trypho said, "Ask the questions." Then I said, "Do you think that any other one is said to be worthy of worship and called Lord and God in the Scriptures, except the Maker of all, and Christ, who by so many Scriptures was proved to you to have become man?" (232)

And since they are compelled, they agree that some Scriptures which we mention to them, and which expressly prove that Christ was to suffer, to be worshipped, and [to be called] God. (233)

And by which this very man who was crucified is proved to have been set forth expressly as God and man. (234)

Moreover, in the book of Exodus we have also perceived that the name of God Himself which, He says, was not revealed to Abraham or to Jacob, was Jesus, and was declared mysteriously through Moses. Thus it is written: 'And the Lord spake to Moses, Say to this people, Behold, I send My angel before thy face, to keep thee in the way, to bring thee into the land which I have prepared for thee. Give heed to Him and obey Him; do not disobey Him. For He will not draw back from you; for My name is in Him. (236)

Now understand that He who led your fathers into the land is called by this name Jesus, and first called Auses. (236)

If, then, we know that God revealed Himself in so many forms to Abraham, and to Jacob, and to Moses. (236)

But we are able to prove that it happened in the case of our Christ. For at the time of His birth, Magi who came from Arabia worshipped Him. (237)

Just as Eve was made from one of Adam's ribs, and as all living beings were created in the beginning by the word of God. (241)

And Jacob, having poured oil on a stone in the same place, is testified to by the very God who appeared to him, that he had anointed a pillar to the God who appeared to him. And that the stone symbolically proclaimed Christ. (242)

'Therefore God, even Thy God, hath anointed Thee with the oil of gladness above Thy fellows.' (242)

For the former gave them a temporary inheritance, seeing he was neither Christ who is God. (255)

Now I have proved at length that Christ is called God. (262)

"It is written, Thou shalt worship the Lord thy God, and Him only shall thou serve." (262)

The various names of Christ according to both natures. It is shown that He is God and appeared to the patriarchs. (262)

"But if you knew, Trypho," continued I, "who He is that is called at one time the Angel of great counsel, and a Man by Ezekiel, and like the Son of man by Daniel, and a Child by Isaiah, and Christ and God to be worshipped by David, and Christ and a Stone by many, and Wisdom by Solomon, and Joseph and Judah and a Star by Moses, and the East by Zechariah, and the Suffering One and

Jacob and Israel by Isaiah again, and a Rod, and Flower, and Corner-Stone, and Son of God." (262)

For if you had understood what has been written by the prophets, you would not have denied that He was God, Son of the only, unbegotten, unutterable God. (263)

And also, of Christ, but [saw] Him who was according to His will His Son, being God, and the Angel because He ministered to His will; whom also it pleased Him to be born man by the Virgin; who also was fire when He conversed with Moses from the bush. (263)

For he who knows not Him, knows not the will of God; and he who insults and hates Him, insults and hates Him that sent Him. And whoever believes not in Him, believes not the declarations of the prophets, who preached and proclaimed Him to all. (268)

And I, praying for them, said, "I can wish no better thing for you, sirs, than this, that, recognizing in this way that intelligence is given to every man, you may be of the same opinion as ourselves, and believe that Jesus is the Christ of God." (270)

In *Ante-Nicene Fathers*, volume 1, in "Justin's Hortatory Address to the Greeks," Justin Martyr wrote,

And God, the Father of the universe, who is the perfect intelligence, is the truth. And the Word, being His Son, came to us, having put on flesh, revealing both Himself and the Father, giving to us in Himself resurrection from the dead, and eternal life afterwards. And this is Jesus Christ, our Saviour and Lord. He, therefore, is Himself both the faith and the proof of Himself and of all things Wherefore those who follow Him, and know Him, having faith in Him as their proof, shall rest in Him. (294)

In *Ante-Nicene Fathers*, volume 1, in Ireneus's "Against Heresies" Ireneus wrote,

> And in what respect will the Word of God—yea, rather God Himself since He is the Word. (375)

> Therefore neither would the Lord, nor the Holy Spirit, nor the apostles, have ever named as God, definitely and absolutely, him who was not God, unless he were truly God; nor would they have named any one in his own person Lord, except God the Father ruling over all, and His Son who has received dominion from His Father over all creation. (418)

> Since, therefore, the Father is truly Lord, and the Son truly Lord, the Holy Spirit has fitly designated them by the title of Lord. (418)

> For the Spirit designates both [of them] by the name, of God—both Him who is anointed as Son, and Him who does anoint, that is, the Father. (419)

In *Ante-Nicene Fathers*, volume 1, in Ireneus's "Against Heresies," book III, he wrote:

> But these are the Church. For she is the synagogue of God, which God—that is, the Son Himself—has gathered by Himself." (419)

> Who is meant by God? He of whom He has said, "God shall come openly, our God, and shall not keep silence; "that is, the Son, who came manifested to men who said." (419)

> Wherefore, as I have already stated, no other is named as God, or is called Lord, except Him who is God and Lord of all, who also said to Moses, "I AM THAT I AM." (419)

Therefore, God has been declared through the Son, who is in the Father, and has the Father in Himself—He who is, the Father bearing witness to the Son, and the Son announcing the Father. (419)

"Behold, a virgin shall conceive, and shall bring forth a son, and they shall call his name Emmanuel; which is, being interpreted, God with us." (422)

"Of whose kingdom is no end;" and frankincense, because He was God, who also "was made known in Judea," and was "declared to those who sought Him not." (423)

"The Spirit of God is upon Me, because He hath anointed Me: He hath sent Me to preach the Gospel to the lowly, to heal the broken up in heart, to proclaim liberty to the captives, and sight to the blind; to announce the acceptable year of the Lord, and the day of vengeance; to comfort all that mourn." For inasmuch as the Word of God was man from the root of Jesse, and son of Abraham, in this respect did the Spirit of God rest upon Him and anoint Him to preach the Gospel to the lowly. But inasmuch as He was God. (423)

The disciple of the Lord therefore desiring to put an end to all such doctrines, and to establish the rule of truth in the Church, that there is one Almighty God, who made all things by His Word, both visible and invisible; showing at the same time, that by the Word, through whom God made the creation, He also bestowed salvation on the men included in the creation; thus commenced His teaching in the Gospel: "In the beginning was the Word, and the Word was with God, and the WORD was God. The same was in the beginning with God. All things were made by Him, and without Him was nothing made." (226)

For "no man," he says, "hath seen God at any time," unless "the only-begotten Son of God, which is in the bosom of the Father, He hath declared [Him]." For He, the Son who is in His bosom, declares to all the Father who is invisible. Wherefore they know Him to whom the Son reveals Him; and again, the Father, by means of the Son, gives knowledge of His Son to those who love Him." (427)

But that there was one and the same God the Father, and Christ Jesus who rose from the dead; and they preached faith in Him. (430)

This is the mystery which he says was made known to him by revelation, that He who suffered under Pontius Pilate, the same is Lord of all, and King and God, and Judge, receiving power from Him who is the God of all, because He became "obedient unto death, even the death of the cross." (433)

When Paul says, "How beautiful are the feet of those bringing glad tidings of good things, and preaching the Gospel of peace, he shows clearly that it was not merely one, but there were many who used to preach the truth. And again, in the Epistle to the Corinthians, when he had recounted all those who had seen God after the resurrection, he says in continuation, "But whether it were I or they, so we preach, and so ye believed," acknowledging as one and the same, the preaching of all those who saw God after the resurrection from the dead. (437)

The Lord replied to Philip, who wished to behold the Father, "Have I been so long a time with you, and yet thou hast not known Me, Philip? He that sees Me, sees also the Father; and how sayest thou then, Show us the Father? "For I am in the Father, and the Father is in Me; and henceforth ye know Him, and have seen Him." To these men, therefore, did the Lord bear witness, that in Himself, they had both known and seen the Father (and the Father is truth)." (437)

But in every respect, too, He is man, the formation of God; and thus He took up man into Himself, the invisible becoming visible, the incomprehensible being made comprehensible, the impassible becoming capable of suffering, and the Word being made man, thus summing up all things in Himself: so that as in super-celestial, spiritual, and invisible things, the Word of God is supreme, so also in things visible and corporeal He might possess the supremacy, and, taking to Himself the pre-eminence, as well as constituting Himself Head of the Church, He might draw all things to Himself at the proper time. (443)

But when the fullness of time came, God sent forth His Son. By which is made manifest, that all things which had been foreknown of the Father, our Lord did accomplish in their order, season, and hour, foreknown and fitting, being indeed one and the same, but rich and great. For He fulfils the bountiful and comprehensive will of His Father, inasmuch as He is Himself the Saviour of those who are saved, and the Lord of those who are under authority, and the God of all those things which have been formed, the only-begotten of the Father, Christ who was announced, and the Word of God, who became incarnate when the fullness of time had come, at which the Son of God had to become the Son of man. (443)

[Namely,] that the Spirit of God as a dove descended upon Him; this Spirit, of whom it was declared by Isaiah, "And the Spirit of God shall rest upon Him," (444)

The Spirit, therefore, descending under the predestined dispensation, and the Son of God, the Only-begotten, who is also the Word of the Father. (445)

For it was incumbent upon the Mediator between God and men, by His relationship to both, to bring both to friendship and, concord, and present man to God, while He revealed God to man. (448)

Thus, then, was the Word of God made man. (448)

But what He did appear, that He also was: God recapitulated in Himself the ancient formation of man, that He might kill sin, deprive death of its power, and vivify man, and therefore His works are true. (448)

Jesus Christ was not a mere man, begotten from Joseph in the ordinary course of nature, but was very God, begotten of the Father most high, and very man, born of the Virgin. (448)

For I have shown from the Scriptures, that no one of the sons of Adam is as to everything, and absolutely, called God, or named Lord. But that He is Himself in His own right, beyond all men who ever lived, God, and Lord, and King Eternal, and the Incarnate Word, proclaimed by all the prophets, the apostles and by the Spirit Himself, may be seen by all who have attained to even a small portion of the truth. (449)

He is the holy Lord, the Wonderful, the Counselor, the Beautiful in appearance, and the Mighty God, coming on the clouds as the Judge of all men; —all these things did the Scriptures prophesy of Him. (449)

That it is from that region which is towards the south of the inheritance of Judah that the Son of God shall come, who is God, and who was from Bethlehem. (451)

God, then, was made man, and the Lord did Himself save us. (451)

And as the protoplast himself Adam, had his substance from untilled and as yet virgin soil ("for God had not yet sent rain, and man had not tilled the ground,") and was formed by the hand of God, that is, by the Word of God, for "all things were made by Him. (454)

Ireneus wrote in "Against Heresies," book IV,

He is the God of the living; and His Word is He who also spake to Moses. (467)

Christ Himself, therefore, together with the Father, is the God of the living, who spake to Moses, and who was also manifested to the fathers. (467)

For by means of the creation itself, the Word reveals God the Creator; and by means of the world [does He declare] the Lord the Maker of the world; and by means of the formation [of man] the Artificer who formed him. (469)

And through the Word Himself who had been made visible and palpable, was the Father shown forth, although all did not equally believe in Him; but all saw the Father in the Son: for the Father is the inviible of the Son, but the Son the visible of the Father. (469)

And for this reason, all spake with Christ when He was present [upon earth], and they named Him God. (469)

No man knoweth the Father, "but one and the same, the Father making all things subject to Him; while He received testimony from all that He was very man, and that He was very God, from the Father, from the Spirit, from angels, from the creation itself, from men, from apostate spirits and demons, from the enemy, and last of all, from death itself." (469)

But the Son is the knowledge of the Father; but the knowledge of the Son is in the Father, and has been revealed through the Son; and this was the reason why the Lord declared: "No man knoweth the Son, but the Father; nor the Father, save the Son, and those to whomsoever the Son shall reveal [Him]." For "shall reveal" was said not with reference to the future alone, as if then [only] the Word had begun to manifest the Father when He was born of Mary, but it applies indifferently throughout all time. For the Son, being present with His own handiwork from the beginning, reveals the Father to all; to whom He wills, and when He wills, and as the Father wills. (469)

Not with reference to the future alone, as if then [only] the Word had begun to manifest the Father when He was born of Mary, but it applies indifferently throughout all time. For the Son, being present with His own handiwork from the beginning, reveals the Father to all; to whom He wills, and when He wills, and as the Father wills. (469)

Therefore, Abraham also, knowing the Father through the Word, who made heaven and earth, confessed Him to be God. (469)

He is therefore one and the same God, who called Abraham and gave him the promise. (470)

But the Son reveals the Father to all to whom He wills that He should be known; and neither without the goodwill of the Father nor without the agency of the Son, can any man know God. (470)

The prophets, then, indicated beforehand that God should be seen by men. (489)

He is, [God] is invisible and indescribable to all things which have been made by Him, but He is by no means unknown: for all things learn through His Word that there is one God the Father, who contains all things, and who grants existence to all. (489)

And for this reason, did the Word become the dispenser of the paternal grace for the benefit of men, for whom He made such great dispensations, revealing God indeed to men, but presenting man to God, and preserving at the same time the invisibility of the Father. (489)

For at one time He was seen with those who were around Ananias, Azarias, Misael, as present with them in the furnace of fire, in the burning, and preserving them from [the effects of] fire: "And the appearance of the fourth," it is said, "was like to the Son of God." (491)

Irenaeus wrote in "Against Heresies," book V,

Now, that the Word of God forms us in the womb, He says to Jeremiah, "Before I formed thee in the womb." (543)

True knowledge, then, consists in the understanding of Christ, which Paul terms the wisdom of God hidden in a mystery. (574)

The sacred books acknowledge with regard to Christ, that as He is the Son of man, so is the same Being not a [mere] man; and as He is flesh, so is He also spirit, and the Word of God, and God. (576)

With regard to Christ, the law and the prophets and the evangelists have proclaimed that He was born of a virgin, that He suffered upon a beam of wood, and that He appeared from the dead; that He also ascended to the heavens, and was glorified by the Father, and is the Eternal King; that He is the perfect Intelligence, the Word of God, who was begotten before the light; that He was the Founder of the universe, along with it (light), and the Maker of man; that He is All in all: Patriarch among the patriarchs; Law in the laws; Chief Priest among priests; Ruler among kings; the Prophet among prophets; the Angel among angels; the Man among men; Son in the Father; Son in the Father; God in God; King to all eternity. For it is He who sailed [in the ark] along with Noah, and who guided Abraham; who was bound along with Isaac, and was a Wanderer with Jacob; the Shepherd of those who are saved, and the Bridegroom of the Church; the Chief also of the cherubim, the Prince of the angelic powers; God of God; Son of the Father; Jesus Christ; King for ever and ever. Amen. (577)

Ante-Nicene Fathers, volume 2, contains Tatian's "Address to the Greeks." (59) Tatian wrote,

God was in the beginning; but the beginning, we have been taught, is the power of the Logos. (67)

We do not act as fools, O Greeks, nor utter idle tales, when we announce that God was born in the form of a man. (74)

Theophilus to Autolycus, in book I (85), wrote, "But what else is this voice but the Word of God, who is also His Son? ... The Word, then, being God. (103)

Ante-Nicene Fathers, volume 2—Clement of Alexandria wrote in his "Exhortation to the Heathens,"

> This Word, then, the Christ, the cause of both our being at first (for He was in God) and of our well-being, this very Word has now appeared as man, He alone being both, both God and man—the Author of all blessings to us; by whom we, being taught to live well, are sent on our way to life eternal. This is the New Song, 868 the manifestation of the Word that was in the beginning, and before the beginning. The Saviour, who existed before, has in recent days appeared. He, who is in Him that truly is, has appeared; for the Word, who "was with God," and by whom all things were created, has appeared as our Teacher. The Word, who in the beginning bestowed on us life as Creator when He formed us, taught us to live well when He appeared as our Teacher; that as God He might afterwards conduct us to the life which never ends. (173)

> And will show what we could not have known before, had we not entered in by Christ, through whom alone God is beheld. (174)

> But are ye so devoid of fear, or rather of faith, as not to believe the Lord Himself, or Paul, who in Christ's stead thus entreats: "Taste and see that Christ is God?" (196)

> Believe Him who is man and God; believe, O man. Believe, O man, the living God, who suffered and is adored. Believe, ye slaves, Him who died; believe, all ye of human kind, Him who alone is God of all men. (201)

Thou leadest me to the light, O Lord, and I find God through Thee, and receive the Father from Thee, I become "Thy fellow-heir." (203)

Clement of Alexandria wrote in "The Instructor" (208),

Now, O you, my children, our Instructor is like His Father God, whose son He is, sinless, blameless, and with a soul devoid of passion; God in the form of man, stainless, the minister of His Father's will, the Word who is God, who is in the Father, who is at the Father's right hand, and with the form of God is God. (210)

The Lord ministers all good and all help, both as man and as God: as God, forgiving our sins; and as man, training us not to sin. (210)

And His name has been called the Angel of great Counsel. Who, then, is this infant child? He according to whose image we are made little children. By the same prophet is declared His greatness: "Wonderful, Counselor, Mighty God, Everlasting Father, Prince of Peace; that He might fulfill His discipline: and of His peace there shall be no end." O the great God! O the perfect child! The Son is in the Father, and the Father is in the Son. (215)

For since Scripture calls the infant children lambs, it has also called Him God the Word who became man for our sakes. (215)

But our Instructor is the holy God Jesus, the Word, who is the guide of all humanity. The loving God Himself is our Instructor. (223)

Again, when He speaks in His own person, He confesses Himself to be the Instructor: "I am the Lord thy God, who brought thee out of the land of Egypt." Who, then, has the power of leading in and out? Is it not the Instructor? This was He who appeared to Abraham, and said to him, "I am thy God, be accepted before Me." (223)

Now that the Word was at once Jacob's trainer and the Instructor of humanity [appears from this]— He asked, It is said, "His name, and said to him, tell me what Thy name is." And he said, "Why is it that thou askest My name?" For He reserved the new name for the new people—the babe; and was as yet unnamed, the Lord God not having yet become man. Yet Jacob called the name of the place, "Face of God." "For I have seen," he says, "God face to face; and my life is preserved. The face of God is the Word by whom God is manifested and made known." (224)

In the person of Jesus, by whom also, as by even scales, we know God. (227)

Very clearly, then, we conclude Him to be one and the same God. (227)

Wherefore also Paul says, "But now the righteousness of God without the law is manifested;" and again, that you may better conceive of God, "even the righteousness of God by the faith of Jesus Christ upon all that believe; for there is no difference." (228)

So that from this it is clear, that one alone, true, good, just, in the image and likeness of the Father, His Son Jesus, the Word of God, is our Instructor; to whom God hath entrusted us. (234)

"All Wisdom is from the Lord, and with Him for evermore;"—with authority of utterance, for He is God and Creator: "For all things were made by Him, and without Him was not anything made." (234)

For the Word Himself is the manifest mystery: God in man, and man God. And the Mediator executes the Father's will; for the Mediator is the Word, who is common to both—the Son of God, the Savior of men. (271)

Clement of Alexandria wrote in "The Stromata, or Miscellanie," book I,

But the teaching, which is according to the Savior, is complete in itself and without defect, being "the power and wisdom of God. (323)

And John the apostle says: "No man hath seen God at any time. The only-begotten God, who is in the bosom of the Father, He hath declared Him," calling invisibility and ineffableness the bosom of God. (463)

Ante-Nicene Fathers, volume 2—Clemens Alexandrinus, "On The Salvation of the Rich Man," writes,

For He foresaw as God, both what He would be asked, and what each one would answer Him. (593)

For what further need has God of the mysteries of love? And then thou shalt look into the bosom of the Father, whom God the only begotten Son alone hath declared. (601)

In *Ante-Nicene Fathers*, volume 3, Tertullian wrote in "Apology,"

We have been taught that He proceeds forth from God, and in that procession, He is generated; so that He is the Son of God and is called God from unity of substance with God. For God, too, is a Spirit. Even when the ray is shot from the sun, it is still part of the parent mass; the sun will still be in the ray, because it is a ray of the sun—there is no division of substance, but merely an extension. Thus Christ is Spirit of Spirit, and God of God, as light of light is kindled. (34)

In this way, also, Christ is Spirit of Spirit, and God of God. (34)

We say, and before all men we say, and torn and bleeding under your tortures, we cry out, "We worship God through Christ." Count Christ a man, if you please; by Him and in Him God would be known and be adored. (36)

Tertullian, in "An Answer to the Jews," wrote,

What shall I say of the Romans themselves, who fortify their own empire with garrisons of their own legions, nor can extend the might of their kingdom beyond these nations? But Christ's Name is extending everywhere, believed everywhere, worshipped by all the above-enumerated nations, reigning everywhere, adored everywhere, conferred equally everywhere upon all No king, with Him, finds greater favor, no barbarian lesser joy; no dignities or pedigrees enjoy distinctions of merit; to all He is equal, to all King, to all Judge, to all "God and Lord." (158)

Therefore, God Himself will give you a sign; Behold, the virgin shall conceive, and bear a son, and ye shall call his name Emmanuel (which is, interpreted, "God with us"). (161)

Tertullian, in "A Treatise on the Soul," wrote,

It is not to the Philosophers that We Resort for Information about the Soul But to God. ... So that all the wisdom of Socrates, at that moment, proceeded from the affectation of an assumed composure, rather than the firm conviction of ascertained truth. For by whom has truth ever been discovered without God? By whom has God ever been found without Christ? (181)

For God alone is without sin; and the only man without sin; is Christ, since Christ is also God. (221)

In "The Prescription against Heretics," Tertullian wrote, "Christ Jesus our Lord (may He bear with me a moment in thus expressing myself!), whosoever He is, of what God so ever He is the Son, of what substance so ever He is man and God." (252).

Tertullian, in "Against Marcion," book II, wrote,

Inasmuch as ye yourselves have now come to the belief that God moved about in the form and all other circumstances of man's nature, you will of course no longer require to be convinced that God conformed Himself to humanity. (318)

It is He who descends, He who interrogates, He who demands, He who swears. With regard, however, to the Father, the very gospel which is common to us will testify that He was never visible according to the word of Christ: "No man knoweth the Father, save the Son." For even in the Old Testament He had declared, "No man shall see me, and live." He means that the Father is invisible, in whose authority and in whose name was He God who appeared as the Son of God. (318–319)

But with us Christ is received in the person of Christ, because even in this manner is He our God Whatever attributes therefore you require as worthy of God, must be found in the Father, who is invisible and unapproachable, and placid, and (so to speak) the God of the philosophers; whereas those qualities which you censure as unworthy must be supposed to be in the Son, who has been seen, and heard, and encountered, the Witness and Servant of the Father, uniting in Himself man and God. (319)

But the Scripture offers me further information, even in the interpretation of the Lord Himself. For when the Jews, who looked at Him as merely man, and were not yet sure that He was God also, as being likewise the Son of God, rightly enough said that a man could not forgive sins, but God alone. (359)

By God, however, would that be done which the man Christ was to do, for He was likewise God. (363)

That you may know how Gentiles then flocked to Him, because He was born the God-man who was to build the church according to the Father's will—even of other races also. (365)

He would have said that no such faith had ever had existence in Israel; but as the case stands, He intimates that He ought to have found so great a faith in Israel, inasmuch as He had indeed come for the purpose of finding it, being in truth the God and Christ of Israel. (375)

He adds: "But if I with the finger of God cast out demons is not the kingdom of God come near unto you?" For the magicians who stood before Pharaoh and resisted Moses called the power of the Creator "the finger of God." (393)

This Christ also showed, when, recalling to notice (and no obliterating) those ancient wonders which were really His own, He said that the power of God must be understood to be the finger of none other God than Him, under whom it had received this appellation. (390)

It follows that the apostle, when treating of the Creator, (as Him whom both Jew and Gentile as yet have) not known, means undoubtedly to teach us, that the God who is to become known (in Christ) is the Creator. (439)

Their sound is gone out through all the earth, and their words to the end of the world. He calls Christ "the image of the invisible God." We in like manner say that the Father of Christ is invisible, for we know that it was the Son who was seen in ancient times (whenever any appearance was vouchsafed to men in the name of God) as the image of (the Father) Himself. (470)

It is well for us that in another passage (the apostle) calls Christ "the image of the invisible God." ... But since he is truly God ... Therefore, as He was found to be God by His mighty power, so was He found to be man by reason of His flesh, because the apostle could not have pronounced Him to have "become obedient unto death," if He had not been constituted of a mortal substance. (473)

In "Against Hermogenes," Tertullian wrote, "Because the Son is the Word," and "the Word is God," and "I and my Father are one" (488).

Tertullian, in "On the Flesh of Christ," wrote,

The expression is in the singular number, as referring to the Lord, "He was born of God." And very properly, because Christ is the Word of God, and with the Word the spirit of God, and by the Spirit the Power of God, and whatsoever else appertains to God. (538)

In speaking of the apostle Paul and what he wrote to Timothy, Tertullian quotes from the New Testament.

He charges Timothy himself "to keep what had been committed to his care, without spot, unrebukable, until the appearing of the Lord Jesus Christ: which in His times He shall show, who is the blessed and only Potentate, the King of kings and Lord of lords," speaking of (Him as) God." (562)

The Acts of the Apostles, too, attest the resurrection. Now the apostles had nothing else to do, at least among the Jews, than to explain the Old Testament and confirm the New, and above all, to preach God in Christ. (573)

Tertullian, in "Against Praxeas," wrote,

But I shall follow the apostle; so that if the Father and the Son, are alike to be invoked, I shall call the Father "God," and invoke Jesus Christ as, "Lord." But when Christ alone (is mentioned), I shall be able to call Him "God," as the same apostle says: "Of whom is Christ, who is over all, God blessed forever." (608)

It will therefore follow, that by Him who is invisible we must understand the Father in the fullness of His majesty, while we recognize the Son visible by reason of the dispensation of His derived existence; We declare, however, that the Son also, considered in Himself (as the Son), is invisible, in that He is God, and the Word and Spirit of God; but that He was visible before the days of His flesh. (609)

Believe that there is one only God, but under the following dispensation, or οἰκονομία, as it is called, that this one only God has also a Son, His Word, who proceeded from Himself, by whom all things were made, and without whom nothing was made. Him we believe to have been sent by the Father into the Virgin, and to have been born of her—being both Man and God, the Son of Man and the Son of God. (598)

That when Christ should come He might be both acknowledged as God and designated as Lord, being the Son of Him who is both God and Lord. (608)

We declare, however, that the Son also, considered in Himself (as the Son), is invisible, in that He is God, and the Word and Spirit of God; but that He was visible before the days of His flesh, in the way that He says to Aaron and Miriam, "And if there shall be a prophet amongst you, I will make myself known to him in a vision, and will speak to him in a dream; not as with Moses, with whom I shall speak mouth to mouth, even apparently, that is to say, in truth, and not enigmatically, "that is to say, in image." (609)

He is God of God. (610–611)

Did Paul behold; but he saw not the Father. "Have I not," he says, "seen Jesus Christ our Lord?" Moreover, he expressly called Christ God, saying: "Of whom are the fathers, and of whom as concerning the flesh Christ came, who is over all, God blessed forever." (611)

When, therefore, you read of Almighty God, and the Most High, and the God of hosts, and the King of Israel, the "One that is," consider whether the Son also be not indicated by these designations, who in His own right is God Almighty, in that He is the Word of Almighty God, and has received power over all. (613)

He which is to come were not almighty; whereas even the Son of the Almighty is as much almighty as the Son of God is God. (613)

He is entitled to be called God ... Lord's answer to Philip, "I and my Father are one;" and, "He that hath seen me hath seen the Father; and I am in the Father, and the Father in me." (615)

The Jews sought the more intently to kill Him, not only because He broke the Sabbath, but also because He said that God was His Father, thus making Himself equal with God. (616)

Since God became man in the midst of it and established it by the will of the Father. ... The Word is God, and "the Word of the Lord, remaineth forever." (623)

But the truth is, we find that He is expressly set forth as both God and Man; the very psalm which we have quoted intimating (of the flesh), that "God became Man in the midst of it, He therefore established it by the will of the Father,"—certainly in all respects as the Son of God and the Son of Man, being God and Man, differing no doubt according to each substance in its own especial property, inasmuch as the Word is nothing else but God, and the flesh nothing else but Man. (624)

In "On Prayer," Tertullian continues,

To us it has been revealed in the Son, for the Son is now the Father's new name. (682)

We, however, pray to the Lord ... We, however, not only raise, but even expand them; and, taking our model from the Lord's passion even in prayer we confess to Christ. (685)

This bodily patience adds a grace to our prayers for good, a strength to our prayers against evil; this opens the ears of Christ our God. (715)

In *Ante-Nicene Fathers*, volume 4, in Origen De Principiis's preface, he wrote,

> And by the words of Christ we do not mean those only which He spake when He became man and tabernacled in the flesh; for before that time, Christ, the Word of God, was in Moses and the prophets. For without the Word of God, how could they have been able to prophesy of Christ? (239)

> Secondly, That Jesus Christ Himself, who came (into the world), was born of the Father before all creatures; that, after He had been the servant of the Father in the creation of all things—"For by Him were all things made" He in the last times, divesting Himself (of His glory), became a man, and was incarnate although God, and while made a man remained the God which He was. (240)

> On God in Thy word and wisdom which is Thy Son, in Himself we shall see Thee the Father. (242)

> If the apostle does not say the same thing, when, speaking of Christ, he declares, that "He is the image of the invisible God, the first-born of every creature." (245)

> And that you may understand that the omnipotence of Father and Son is one and the same, as God and the Lord are one and the same with the Father, listen to the manner in which John speaks in the Apocalypse: "Thus saith the Lord God, which is, and which was, and which is to come, the Almighty." (250)

In Origen De Principiis's book IV, he wrote,

> It shows that God, having really become man, delivered to men the doctrines of salvation. (351)

And to the house of David has been given a sign: for the Virgin bore, and was pregnant, and brought forth a son, and His name is Emmanuel, which is, "God with us;" and as the same prophet says, the prediction has been fulfilled, "God (is) with us; know it, O nations, and be overcome." (352)

But it was, as the prophets also predicted, from a virgin that there was to be born, according to the promised sign, one who was to give His name to the fact, showing that at His birth God was to be with man. Now it seems to me appropriate to the character of a Jew to have quoted the prophecy of Isaiah, which says that Immanuel was to be born of a virgin. (410–411)

And the prediction runs thus: "And the Lord spake again unto Ahaz, saying, Ask thee a sign of the LORD thy God; ask it either in the depth or in the height above. But Ahaz said, I will not ask, neither will I tempt the LORD. And he said, Hear ye now, O house of David; is it a small thing for you to weary men, but will ye weary my God also? Therefore, the Lord Himself shall give you a sign. Behold, a virgin shall conceive, and bear a son, and shall call His name Immanuel, which is, being interpreted, God with us." (411)

But attend carefully to what follows, where He is called God: "For Thy throne, O God, is for ever and ever: a sceptre of righteousness is the sceptre of Thy kingdom." (421)

He possessed within that form which was seen by the eyes of men some higher element of divinity,—that which was properly the Son of God—God the Word— the power of God, and the wisdom of God—He who is called the Christ. (426)

We therefore charge the Jews with not acknowledging Him to be God, to whom testimony was borne in many passages by the prophets, to the effect that He was a mighty power, and a God next to the God and Father of all things. (433)

Now, on this head we have briefly replied to the charges of Celsus in the preceding pages, where Christ was shown to be the first-born of all creation, who assumed a body and a human soul; and that God gave commandment respecting the creation of such mighty things in the world, and they were created; and that He who received the command was God the Logos. (444)

You, O sincere believers, find fault with us, because we do not recognize this individual as God. (446)

But since he has charged us, I know not how often already, "with regarding this Jesus, who was but a mortal body, as a God." (480)

As Paul also taught in his address to the Athenians; and therefore, although the God of the universe should through His own power descend with Jesus into the life of men, and although the Word which was in the beginning with God, which is also God Himself. (499)

Now the answer to these statements might have respect partly to the nature of the Divine Word, who is God. (504)

And may God grant, through His Son, who is God the Word, and Wisdom, and Truth, and Righteousness, and everything else which the sacred Scriptures when speaking of God call Him. (541)

Because you do not assent to the dictum of Celsus, that "neither has a God nor the son of a God come down nor is to come down to mankind," why not rather carefully ascertain from the statements made regarding Jesus, and the prophecies uttered concerning Him, who it is that we are to consider as having come down to the human race as God, and the Son of God? (543)

For every prayer, and supplication, and intercession, and thanksgiving, is to be sent up to the Supreme God through the High Priest, who is above all the angels, the living Word and God. And to the Word Himself shall we also pray and make intercessions, and offer thanksgivings and supplications to Him. (544)

But that for a good end we listen to the God who speaks in Moses, and have accepted Jesus, whom he testifies to be God, as the Son of God, but that for a good end we listen to the God who speaks in Moses, and have accepted Jesus, whom he testifies to be God, as the Son of God. (566)

If Celsus were to ask us how we think we know God, and how we shall be saved by Him, we would answer that the Word of God, which entered into those who seek Him, or who accept Him when He appears, is able to make known and to reveal the Father, who was not seen (by any one) before the appearance of the Word. And who else is able to save and conduct the soul of man to the God of all things, save God the Word, who, "being in the beginning with God," became flesh for the sake of those who had cleaved to the flesh, and had become as flesh, that He might be received by those who could not behold Him, inasmuch as He was the Word, and was with God, and was God?" (604)

Moreover, that these words, "He that hath seen Me, hath seen the Father who sent Me," are not to be taken in their grosser sense, is plain from the answer which He gave to Philip, "Have I been so long time with you, and yet dost thou not know Me, Philip?" after Philip had asked, "Show us the Father, and it sufficeth us. "He, then, who perceives how these words, "The Word was made flesh," are to be understood of the only-begotten Son of God, the first-born of all creation, will also understand how, in seeing the image of the invisible God, we see "the Creator and Father of the universe." (628)

But he prays for no trivial blessings, for he has learnt from Jesus to seek for nothing small or mean, that is, sensible objects, but to ask only for what is great and truly divine; and these things God grants to us, to lead us to that blessedness which is found only with Him through His Son, the Word, who is God. Simplest of Christians, who lead, however, a life of greater moderation and purity than many philosophers—"to confound the wise." (629)

To explain this fully, and to justify the conduct of the Christians in refusing homage to any object except the Most High God, and the First-born of all creation, who is His Word and God, we must quote this from Scripture. (639)

For the Lord of those who are "ambassadors for Christ" is Christ Himself, whose ambassadors they are, and who is, "the Word, who was in the beginning, was with God, and was God." (642)

And we do not "reverence beyond measure one who has but lately appeared," as though He did not exist before; for we believe Himself when He says, "Before Abraham was, I am." Again, He says, "I am the truth;" and surely none of us is so simple as to suppose that truth did not exist before the time when Christ appeared. We worship, therefore, the Father of truth, and the Son, who is the truth; and these, while they are two, considered as persons or subsistence's, are one in unity of thought, in harmony and in identity of will. So entirely are they one, that he who has seen the Son, "who is the brightness of God's glory, and the express image of His person," has seen in Him who is the image of God, God Himself. (643)

Thus the Spirit of Christ dwells in those who bear, so to say, a resemblance in form and feature to Himself. And the Word of God, wishing to set this clearly before us, represents God as promising to the righteous, "I will dwell in them, and walk among them; and I will be their God, and they shall be My people." And the Savior says, "If any man hears My words, and do them, I and My Father will come to him, and make Our abode with him." (646)

According to Celsus, then, it would be better for us now to give ourselves up to magic and sorcery than to embrace Christianity, and to put our faith in an innumerable multitude of demons than in the almighty, living, self-revealing God, who has manifested Himself by Him who by His great power has spread the true principles of holiness among all men throughout the world; yea, I may add without exaggeration, He has given this knowledge to all beings everywhere possessed of reason, and needing deliverance from the plague and corruption of sin. (662)

And those who rule over us well are under the constraining influence of the great King, whom we believe to be the Son of God, God the Word. (668)

Ante-Nicene Fathers, volume 5, contains "The Extant Works and Fragments of Hippolytus," part II, in which Hippolytus wrote,

> Now, as our Lord Jesus Christ, who is also God. (206)

> Now, Christ prayed all this economically as man; being, however, true God. (220)

> And that He was sent Peter testifies, when he says to the centurion Cornelius: "God sent His Word unto the children of Israel by the preaching of Jesus Christ. This is the God who is Lord of all." (228)

> He now, coming forth into the world, was manifested as God in a body, coming forth too as a perfect man. For it was not in mere appearance or by conversion, but in truth, that He became man. (230)

> This is the God who for our sakes became man, to whom also the Father hath put all things in subjection To Him to be the glory and the power, with the Father and the Holy Spirit, in the holy Church both now and ever, and even for ever more. Amen. (231)

In "Against Beron and Helix," Hippolytus wrote,

> [Showing Himself thus] as both being in reality and as being understood to be at one and the same time infinite God and finite man. (231)

> The God of all things therefore became truly, according to the Scriptures, without conversion, sinless man, and that in a manner known to Himself alone, as He is the natural Artificer of things which are above our comprehension. (232)

For with this purpose did the God of all things become man, viz., in order that by suffering in the flesh, which is susceptible of suffering, He might redeem our whole race. (232)

He remained therefore, also, after His incarnation, according to nature, God infinite, and more, having the activity proper and suitable to Himself,—an activity growing out of His divinity essentially, and manifested through His perfectly holy flesh by wondrous acts economically, to the intent that He might be believed in as God, while working out of Himself by the flesh, which by nature is weak, the salvation of the universe. (232)

And how will they conceive of the one and the same Christ, who is at once God and man by nature? (233)

It is evident that it also became possessed of the like nature with Him in all wherein that nature consists,—to wit, non-origination, non-generation, infinitude, eternity, incomprehensibility, and whatever else in the way of the transcendent the theological mind discerns in deity. (233)

In "The Discourse on the Holy Theophany," Hippolytus wrote,

We have seen the Creator of all things in the "form of a servant." (235)

A reconciliation took place of the visible with the invisible. (236)

For he who comes down in faith to the laver of regeneration, and renounces the devil, and joins himself to Christ; who denies the enemy, and makes the confession that Christ is God; who puts off the bondage, and puts on the adoption,—he comes up from the baptism brilliant as the sun, flashing forth the beams of righteousness, and, which is indeed the chief thing, he returns a son of God and joint-heir with Christ. (237)

In "Fragments of Discourses or Homilies," Hippolytus wrote,

[The] apostle says, "Even Christ," who is God? (238)

Thus, too, they [prophets] preached of the advent of God in the flesh to the world. (242)

For our God sojourned with us in the flesh. (248)

In the "Appendix to the Works of Hippolytus," he wrote,

And every tongue shall confess Him openly, and shall confess Him who comes to judge righteous judgment, the mighty God and Maker of all things. (252)

Come, ye prophets, who were cast out for my name's sake. Come, ye patriarchs, who before my advent were obedient to me, and longed for my kingdom. (252)

In "The Epistles of Cyprian," Cyprian wrote,

To pray and to entreat the Lord Himself, and then through Him, to make satisfaction to God the Father! We have an advocate and an intercessor for our sins, Jesus Christ the Lord and our God. (286)

Epistle LIX: To deserve well of Christ our Judge and Lord and God. (355)

Epistle LXII: Do not do that which Jesus Christ, our Lord and God. (359)

In "The Treatises of Cyprian," he wrote,

That Christ also is Himself the Word of God. ... That the same is Angel and God. ... That Christ is God. ... Christ our God. ...That Christ is man and God, compounded of either nature, that He might be a mediator between us and the Father. (515)

Also, Paul to the Colossians: "Who is the image of the invisible God, and the first-born of every creature." Also, in the same place: "The first-born from the dead, that He might in all things become the holder of the pre-eminence. ... That the same Christ is the Word of God. (516)

That Christ is at once Angel and God. ... That Christ is God. ... In Genesis: "And God said unto Jacob, Arise, and go up to the place of Bethel, and dwell there; and make there an altar to that God who appeared unto thee. (517)

Of whom, according to the flesh, Christ came, who is God over all, blessed for evermore. ... Also, in the Gospel according to Matthew: "And ye shall call His name Emmanuel, which is, being interpreted, God with us." (518)

That Christ our God should come, the Enlightener and Savior of the human race. ... That this should be the sign of His nativity that He should be born of a virgin— man and God —a son of man and a Son of God. ... That Christ is both man and God, compounded of both natures, that He might be a Mediator between us and the Father. (519)

Also Paul to the Philippians: "Who, being established in the form of God, thought it not robbery that He was equal with God, but emptied Himself, taking the form of a servant, and was made in the likeness of men; and being found in fashion as a man, He humbled Himself, becoming obedient even unto death, even the death of the cross. Wherefore also God exalted Him, and gave Him a name which is above every name, that in the name of Jesus every knee should bow, of things in heaven, of things in earth, things, and every tongue should confess that Jesus Christ is Lord in the glory of God the Father." (521)

Ante-Nicene Fathers, volume 5, contains "Fragments of Caius." Caius was a pupil of Irenaeus. He was a strong opponent against the idea of having a pope. Caius wrote,

I mean Justin and Miltiades Muratorian Canon, and Tatian and Clement, and many others, in all which divinity is ascribed to Christ. For who is ignorant of the books of Irenæus and Melito, and the rest, which declare Christ to be God and man? (601)

For our merciful God and Lord Jesus Christ was not willing that a witness of His own sufferings should perish. (602)

In "A Treatise of Novation Concerning the Trinity," Novation wrote,

Further, that the Same Rule of Truth Teaches Us to Believe, After the Father, Also in the Son of God, Jesus Christ Our Lord God, Being the Same that Was Promised in the Old Testament, and Manifested in the New. (618)

And Indeed, that Christ Was Not Only Man, But God Also; That Even as He Was the Son of Man, So Also He Was the Son of God. ... He is only and alone man, but so as to maintain, by the association of the divinity of the Word in that very materiality, that He was also God according to the Scriptures. ... The argument of divinity in Him gathered from His powers avails to the result also of asserting Him to be God from His works. ... We must not then lean to one side and evade the other side, because any one who should exclude one portion of the truth will never hold the perfect truth. For Scripture as much announces Christ as also God, as it announces God Himself as man. ... It has as much described Jesus Christ to be man, as moreover it has also described Christ the Lord to be God. ... For as nature itself has prescribed that he must be believed to be a man who is of man, so the same nature prescribes also that He must be believed to be God who is of God; but if he should not also be God when he is of God, no more should he be man although he should be of man. ... Jesus is called also God and the Son of God. (620)

And in the same manner as He is born as man subsequent to the world, so as God He is manifested to have been before the world. And in the same way as He was begotten as man of the seed of David, so also the world is said to have been ordained by Him as God. And in the same way as He was as man after many, so as God He was before all. And in the same manner as He was as man inferior to others, so as God He was greater than all. And in the same manner as He ascended as man into heaven, so as God He had first descended thence. ... That Christ is God, is Proved by the Authority of the Old Testament Scriptures. ... Why, then, should man hesitate to call Christ God ... That He is declared to be God by the Father according to the Scriptures? ...

Yea, if God the Father does not save except by God, no one can be saved by God the Father unless he shall have confessed Christ to be God, in whom and by whom the Father promises that He will give him salvation: so that, reasonably, whoever acknowledges Him to be God, may find salvation in Christ God; whoever does not acknowledge Him to be God, would lose salvation which he could not find elsewhere than in Christ God. ... For in the manner that as man He is of Abraham so also as God He is before Abraham himself. ...

So, as God He is found to have all judgment of the quick and dead. ... So, as God He is manifested to have been before the world. ... Behold, a virgin shall conceive and bear a son, and ye shall call His name Emmanuel, which is, interpreted, God with us;" so Christ Himself says, "Lo, I am with you, even to the consummation of the world." Therefore, He is "God with us;" yea, and much rather, He is in us. Christ is with us, therefore it is He whose name is God with us, because He also is with us; or is He not with us? How then does He say that He is with us? He, then, *is* with us. But because He is with us He was called Emmanuel, that is, God with us. God, therefore, because He is with us, was called God with us.

The same prophet says: "Be ye strengthened, ye relaxed hands, and ye feeble knees; be consoled, ye that are cowardly in heart; be strong; fear not. Lo, our God shall return judgment; He Himself shall come, and shall save you ... For, being bound by the words of the prophets, they can no longer deny Christ to be God. ... For now, they cannot deny Him to be God. As God the Father, or as God the Son? (621)

He is the Word of God, who can shrink from declaring without hesitation that He is God. ... The Apostle Thomas, instructed in all the proofs and conditions of Christ's divinity, says in reply to Christ, "My Lord and my God; "and if, besides, the Apostle Paul says, "Whose are the fathers, and of whom Christ came according to the flesh, who is over all, God blessed for evermore." (622)

He is not man only, but God also, since all things are by Him. ... If Christ were only man, being born after John, He could not be before John, unless because He preceded him, in that He is God? ... How does He say that "no man hath seen God at any time, save He which is of God; He hath seen God? ... It was not therefore man that thus came thence from heaven, but the Word of God; that is, God descended thence. (623)

Chapter XV. *Argument.*—Again, He Proves from the Gospel that Christ is God. ... If Christ is only man, how does He say, "Ye are from below, I am from above; ye are of this world, I am not of this world?" ... Therefore, God proceeded from God, in that the Word which proceeded is God, who proceeded forth from God. (624)

But Christ promises to give salvation forever, which if He does not give, He is a deceiver; if He gives, He is God. ... He did not deny Himself to be God, but rather He confirmed the assertion that He was God. ... He proved that He was the Son of God. He is God, therefore, but God in such a manner as to be the Son, not the Father. (625)

And this is life eternal that they should know Thee, the only and true God, and Jesus Christ, whom Thou hast sent?" Had He not wished that He also should be understood to be God, why did He add, "And Jesus Christ, whom Thou hast sent," except because He wished to be received as God also? ... "And the man Jesus Christ, whom Thou hast sent;" but, in fact, He neither added this, nor did Christ deliver Himself to us as man only, but associated Himself with God, as He wished to be understood by this conjunction to be God also, as He is. ... Jesus Christ, who by no means, as we have said, would have linked Himself to the Father had

He not wished to be understood to be God also: for He would have separated Himself from Him had He not wished to be understood to be God. (626)

Moreover Also, from the Fact that He Who Was Seen of Abraham is Called God; Which Cannot Be Understood of the Father, Whom No Man Hath Seen at Any Time; But of the Son in the Likeness of an Angel. (627)

Behold, the same Moses tells us in another place that "God was seen of Abraham." And yet the same Moses hears from God, that "no man can see God and live." If God cannot be seen, how was God seen? Or if He was seen, how is it that He cannot be seen? For John also says, "No man hath seen God at any time;" and the Apostle Paul, "Whom no man hath seen, nor can see." But certainly, the Scripture does not lie; therefore, truly, God was seen. Whence, it may be understood that it was not the Father who was seen, seeing that He never was seen; but the Son, who has both been accustomed to descending, and to be seen because He has descended. For He is the image of the invisible God, as the imperfection and frailty of the human condition was accustomed sometimes even then to see God the Father in the image of God, that is, in the Son of God. (627–628)

Christ also—that is, the image of God, and the Son of God—is looked upon by men, in as much as He could be seen. … Wherefore it is the Son who is seen; but the Son of God is the Word of God: and the Word of God was made flesh and dwelt among us; and this is Christ. What in the world is the reason that we should hesitate to call Him God, who in so many ways is acknowledged to be proved God? … Be remitted to the angel, it was only God the Son, who also is God, who was seen by, Abraham. (628)

But rather Christ, since He is God. ... That God Also Appeared to Jacob as an Angel; Namely, the Son of God. (629)

For I have seen all that Laban hath done to thee. I am God, who appeared to thee in the place of God, where thou anointedst for me there the standing stone. ... And the Angel himself mentions and says, "I am God, who appeared unto thee in the house of God." (630)

"By whom all things were made, and without whom nothing was made;" the imitator of His Father's works and powers, "the image of the invisible God;" "who came down from heaven." (632)

He should be both God of all and should be Lord and be begotten and made known from Himself as God in the form of God the Father. (633)

That divine substance whose name is the Word, whereby all things were made, and without whom nothing was made. For all things are after Him, because they are by Him. And reasonably, He is before all things, but after the Father, since all things were made by Him, and He proceeded from Him of whose will all things were made. Assuredly God proceeding from God. (643)

Thus, the Mediator of God and men, Christ Jesus, having the power of every creature subjected to Him by His own Father, in as much as He is God; with every creature subdued to Him, found at one with His Father God, has, by abiding in that condition that He moreover "was heard," briefly proved God His Father to be one and only and true God. (644)

Ante-Nicene Fathers, volume 6, contains Gregory Thaumaturgus's "The Oration and Panegyric Addressed to Origen." He wrote,

For as He is Himself the Truth, and the Wisdom, and the Power of the Father of the universe, and He is besides in Him, and is truly and entirely made one with Him, it cannot be that, either through forgetfulness or unwisdom, or any manner of infirmity, such as marks one dissociated from Him, He shall either fail in the power to praise Him, or, while having the power, shall willingly neglect (a supposition which it is not lawful, surely, to indulge) to praise the Father. For He alone is able most perfectly to fulfill the whole need of honor which is proper to Him, inasmuch as the Father of all things has made Him one with Himself, and through Him all but completes the circle of His own being objectively, and honors Him with a power in all respects equal to His own, even as also He is honored; which position He first and alone of all creatures that exist has had assigned Him, this Only-begotten of the Father, who is in Him, and who IS God the Word. (24)

And he has become a follower of the unbelief of the Jews, who, supposing the Word of God to be but a human son, have refused to accept Him as God. (41)

Inasmuch as the Son is the Image of God the Father, who is One, —that is, He is God of God; and in like manner the Spirit is called the Spirit of God. ... We therefore acknowledge one true God, the one First Cause, and one Son, very God of very God, possessing of nature the Father's divinity. ... For God, having been incarnated in the flesh of man. ... And it is the true God unincarnate that has appeared incarnate. (44)

For we hold that the Word of God was made man on account of our salvation. ... (We believe therefore in one God, that is, in one First Cause, the God of the law and of the Gospel, the just and good; and in one Lord Jesus

Christ, true God, that is, Image of the true God, Maker of all things seen and unseen. ... One is the Son, both before the incarnation and after the incarnation. The same (Son) is both man and God. (45)

And it is the true God, the unincarnate, that was manifested in the flesh, perfect with the true and divine perfection, not with two natures; nor do we speak of worshipping four (persons), viz., God, and the Son of God, and man, and the Holy Spirit. (47)

IF any one says that the body of Christ is uncreated, and refuses to acknowledge that He, being the uncreated Word (God) of God, took the flesh of, created humanity and appeared incarnate, even as it is written, let him be anathema. ... Yet, while being God, He was recognized as man in a natural manner; and while subsisting truly as man, He was also manifested as God by His works. ... If any one affirms that the flesh of Christ is consubstantial with the divinity, and refuses to acknowledge that He, subsisting Himself in the form of God as God before all ages, emptied Himself and took the form of a servant, even as it is written, let him be anathema. (50)

And if He is the Son of God, then is He also God, of one form with the Father, and co-eternal; in Him the Father possesses all manifestation; He is His image in the person, and through His reflection the (Father's) glory shines forth. ... Namely Christ our God. (59)

It brings us then the glad tidings of that economy of the Savior, which is worthy of all praise, to wit, that, though He was God, He became man through kindness toward man, and did not lay aside, indeed, the dignity which was His from all eternity, but assumed the economy that should work salvation. (63)

For the Christ who was born of the Virgin, and who is our God. … And on this account did God the Word deem it meet to take to Himself the flesh and the perfect humanity by a woman. (65)

I am but a man and am a partaker of the divine grace; but Thou art God, and man to the same effect: for Thou art by nature man's friend. I have need to be baptized of Thee, and comest Thou to me? Thou who wast in the beginning, and wast with God, and wast God. … Thou who art the brightness of the Father's glory; Thou who art the perfect image of the perfect Father. (69)

Ante-Nicene Fathers, volume 6, contains "The Extant Writings of Julius Africanus." We do not have very much personal information about Africanus, but his writing speaks for itself.

Behold, then, the great things that we have told you regarding Christ; and we saw Christ our Savior, who was made known as both God and man. To Him be the glory and the power unto the ages of the ages. Amen. (130)

The Emperor Adrian said: "I shall cause thee to be sacrificed to my gods." The blessed Symphorosa replied: "Thy gods cannot take me in sacrifice; but if I am burned for the name of Christ, my God." (139)

Ante-Nicene Fathers, volume 6, contains "Fragments from the Writings of Peter":

These things and the like, and all the signs which He showed, and His miracles, prove that He is God made man. Both things therefore are demonstrated, that He was God by nature, and that He was man by nature. …

Both therefore is proved, that he was God by nature, and was made man by nature. (280)

Ante-Nicene Fathers, volume 6, contains "Orations Concerning Simeon and Anna," in which Methodius wrote,

> But also the glory to be adored by all, of that one of the sacred Trinity, which now, by the appearance of God in the flesh, hath even lighted upon earth. (384)

> He means, as has been said before, that glorious recognition of our Savior, God in the flesh, who is otherwise invisible to mortal eye. (386)

> Him who is both above and below continuously; Him who is in the form of a servant, and in the form of God the Father. ... I long for Thee, O Lord God of my fathers, and Lord of mercy, who hast deigned, of Thine own glory and goodness, which provides for all, of Thy gracious condescension, with which Thou inclinest towards us, as a Mediator bringing peace, to establish harmony between earth and heaven. I seek Thee, the Great Author of all. With longing I expect Thee who, with Thy word, embracest all things. I wait for Thee, the Lord of life and death. For Thee I look, the Giver of the law, and the Successor of the law. I hunger for Thee, who quickenest the dead; I thirst for Thee, who refreshest the weary; I desire Thee, the Creator and Redeemer of the world.
>
> Thou art our God, and Thee we adore; Thou art our holy Temple, and in Thee we pray; Thou art our Lawgiver, and Thee we obey; Thou art God of all things the First. Before Thee was no other god begotten of God the Father; neither after Thee shall there be any other son consubstantial and of one glory with the Father.

And to know Thee is perfect righteousness, and to know Thy power is the root of immortality.

Thou art He who, for our salvation, was made the head stone of the corner, precious and honorable, declared before to Sion. For all things are placed under Thee as their Cause and Author, as He who brought all things into being out of nothing and gave to what was unstable a firm coherence. ... Thou art fairer than the children of men, who amongst men art very God and man. (387)

What is here present speaks of love to man; what is here apparent, of the Divine condescension. Thankfully, then, receive the God who comes to thee. ... God of Thee begotten, in a manner ineffable, and without corruption, has become man. (388)

And the brightness of the Lord our God hath come down to sojourn with us, so that we see God face to face, and are saved. ... Since by thee the Lord hath appeared, the God of hosts with us. That bush which could not be touched, which beforehand shadowed forth thy figure endowed with divine majesty, bare God without being consumed, who manifested Himself to the prophet just so far as He willed to be seen. (389)

On thy account, and the undefiled Incarnation of God, the Word. ... From which God in human form was made known unto men. (390)

For verily, verily, this prophetic oracle, and most true saying, is concerning thy majesty; for thou alone hast been thought worthy to share with God the things of God; who hast alone borne in the flesh Him, of God the Father was the Eternally and Only-Begotten. So, do they truly believe who hold fast to the pure faith. (391)

Hail, and shine thou Jerusalem, for thy light is come,
the Light Eternal, the Light forever enduring, the
Light Supreme, the Light Immaterial, the Light of one
substance with God and the Father, the Light which is
in the Spirit, and in which is the Father; the Light which
illumines the ages; the Light which gives to mundane
and supramundane things, Christ our very God. (392)

For these thankless men saw, and by means of His
miracles handled the wonder-working God, and yet
remained in unbelief. (395)

Simeon met the Savior and received in his arms, as an
infant, the Creator of the world, and proclaimed Him
to be Lord and God. ... And bless the Lord God seated
upon a colt. ... Blessed is He that cometh in the name
of the Lord! Very God, in the name of the Very God, the
Omnipotent from the Omnipotent, the Son in the name
of the Father. (396)

He is always Lord and God. ... O heretic against the
kingdom of Christ, least thou dishonor Him who begat
Him. If thou art faithful, in faith approach Christ our
very God, and not as using your liberty for a cloak of
maliciousness. (397)

Ante-Nicene Fathers, volume 6, contains "The Seven Books of
Arnobius against the Heathen." Before his conversion to Christianity,
Arnobius, a Christian writer, was a regular person, which means he
went along with the society to which he belonged. I truly appreciate this
kind of Christian, who was a heathen and most likely experienced all
the vices of normal life. Arnobius wrote,

Who has shown us what God is, who He is? ... Is Christ,
then, not to be regarded by us as God? and is He. (423)

He ought to be called and be addressed as God. *But* since He is God in reality and without any shadow of doubt. (424)

And yet it is agreed on that Christ performed all those miracles which He wrought without any aid from external things, without the observance of any ceremonial, without any definite mode of procedure, *but solely* by the inherent might of His authority; and as was the proper duty of *the* true God. (425)

He was God on high, God in His inmost nature, God from unknown realms, and was sent by the Ruler of all as a Savior God. ... He was discovered to be God who heretofore was reckoned one of us? (428)

He is by the confession of all proved to have been God. (429)

Our religion has sprung up just now; for now, He has arrived who was sent to declare it to us, to bring *us* to its truth; to show what God is; to summon us from mere conjectures, to His worship. (462)

Ante-Nicene Fathers, volume 6, contains "The Divine Institutes." In book IV, Lactantius wrote,

But the Greeks speak of Him as the *Logos*, more befittingly than we do as the word, or speech: for *Logos* signifies both speech and reason, in as much as He is both the voice and the wisdom of God. (107)

And when I shall have proved all these things by the writings of those very men who treated with violence their God who had assumed a mortal body. (108)

But He was never called Emmanuel, but Jesus, who in Latin is called Saving, or Savior, because He comes bringing salvation to all nations. But by this name the prophet declared that God incarnate was about to come to men. For Emmanuel signifies God with us; because when He was born of a virgin, men ought to confess that God was with them, that is, on the earth and in mortal flesh. ... Whence David says in the eighty-fourth Psalm, "Truth has sprung out of the earth;" because God, in whom is truth, hath taken a body of earth. (110)

He became both the Son of God through the Spirit, and the Son of man through the flesh,—that is, both God and man. ... But when he acknowledges that He was mortal as to the flesh, which we also declare, it follows that as to the spirit He was God, which we affirm. (112)

What wonder if Apollo thus persuaded men ignorant of the truth, when the Jews also, worshippers (as they seemed to be) of the Most High God, entertained the same opinion, though they had every day before their eyes those miracles which the prophets had foretold to them as about to happen, and yet they could not be induced by the contemplation of such powers to believe that He whom they saw was God? (113)

He received the dignity of everlasting Priest, and the honor of supreme King, and the authority of Judge, and the name of God. (114)

He was therefore both God and man. (126)

For this cause, therefore, a mediator came—that is, God in the flesh. (127)

Therefore we believe Him to be God. (139)

For He is the Deliverer, and Judge, and Avenger, and King, and God, whom we call Christ. (215)

He alone was admitted into a participation of His supreme power, He alone was called God. (238)

It follows that no other hope is proposed to man, unless he shall follow true religion and true wisdom, which is in Christ, and he who is ignorant of Him is always estranged from the truth and from God. Nor let the Jews, or philosophers, flatter themselves respecting the Supreme God. He who has not acknowledged the Son has been unable to acknowledge the Father. This is wisdom, and this is the mystery of the Supreme God. God willed that He should be acknowledged and worshipped through Him. On this account He sent the prophets beforehand to announce His coming, that when the things which had been foretold were fulfilled in Him, then He might be believed by men to be both the Son of God and God. (242)

Ante-Nicene Fathers, volume 7, contains Venantius's "Poem on Easter." Venantius was a little-known Christian writer but still was known as a great Christian writer. Venantius wrote,

Behold, He who was crucified reigns as God over all things, and all created objects offer prayer to their Creator. (329)

But the author of the whole creation is Jesus. His name is the Word; for thus His Father says: "My heart hath emitted a good word." John the evangelist thus says: "In the beginning was the Word, and the Word was with God, and the Word was God. The same was in the beginning with God. All things were made by Him, and without Him was nothing made that was made." Therefore, first, was made the creation; secondly, man, the lord of the human race, as says the apostle. Therefore this Word, when it made light, is called Wisdom; when it made the sky, Understanding; when it made land and sea, Counsel; when it made sun and moon and other bright things, Power; when it calls forth land and sea, Knowledge; when it formed man, Piety; when it blesses and sanctifies man, it has the name of God's fear." (342)

Ante-Nicene Fathers, volume 7, contains the "Introduction Notice to Dionysius, Bishop of Rome." Dionysius, bishop of Rome, a defender of Christian faith and a great Christian, wrote,

> But neither are they less to be blamed who think that the Son was a creation and decided that the Lord was made just as one of those things which really were made; whereas the divine declarations testify that He was begotten, as is fitting and proper, but not that He was created or made. It is therefore not a trifling, but a very great impiety, to say that the Lord was in any wise made with hands. For if the Son was made, there was a time when He was not; but He always was, if, as He Himself declares, He is undoubtedly in the Father. And if Christ is the Word, the Wisdom, and the Power,—for the divine writings tell us that Christ is these, as ye yourselves know, —assuredly these are powers of God. (365)

Ante-Nicene Fathers, volume 7, contains "Early Liturgies." In the "Liturgy of James," he wrote, "Sovereign Lord our God … Sovereign Lord Jesus Christ, O Word of God" (537).

"Our Lord and God, Jesus Christ … O Christ our God … Thy only-begotten Son, our Lord, and God, and Saviour Jesus Christ" (538).

Ante-Nicene Fathers, volume 8, contains "The Testaments of the Twelve Patriarchs":

> And now, my children, obey Levi, and in Judah shall ye be redeemed: and be not lifted up against these two

tribes, for from them shall arise to you the salvation of God. For the Lord shall raise up from Levi as it were a Priest, and from Judah as it were a King, God and man. (12)

Pseudo-Clementine literature offers,

But Christ is God of princes, who is Judge of all. ... Who is God, but the Lord; and who is God, but our Lord? (109)

And since nothing was impossible to Him, He even perceived the thoughts of men, which is possible for none but God only. (145)

Ante-Nicene Fathers, volume 9, contains "The Epistles of Clement," which most likely were the writings of the same person the apostle mentions in Philippians. The apostle says this about Clement:

Indeed, true comrade, I ask you also to help these women who have shared my struggle in the cause of the gospel, together with Clement also, and the rest of my fellow-workers, whose names are in the book of life. (Philippians 4:3)

Brethren, it is fitting that you should think of Jesus Christ as of God,—as the Judge of the living and the dead. (251)

Let us expect, therefore, hour by hour, the kingdom of God in love and righteousness, since we know not the day of the appearing of God. (254)

Ante-Nicene Fathers, volume 9, contains "The Apology of Aristides the Philosopher." Aristides wrote, "The Christians, then, trace the beginning of their religion from Jesus the Messiah; and he is named the Son of God Most High. And it is said that God came down from heaven, and from a Hebrew virgin assumed and clothed himself with flesh" (265).

Volume 9 also contains Origen's "Commentary on the Gospel of John," book I. Origen wrote,

> The Logos was God. ... The Word was God. (320)

> He being the same as the Father. (328)

> So God is able to provide for men a number of occasions, any of which may cause their minds to open to the truth that God, who is over all, has taken on Himself human nature. (342)

> No one hath seen God at any time; the only-begotten God, who is in the bosom of the Father, He hath declared Him. ... For they saw, it may be, the image of the invisible God. (343)

I know you have been overloaded with quotes, but you have just read the greatest of Christian writers. Just by reading these quotes, you have become more informed about Christianity than most Christians or other people will be in their lifetimes. There are a lot more quotes to be read. Remember that this material is not for your reading pleasure but is intended to give you a foundation to live your life in peace and contentment.

I believe the following is some of the greatest material you will ever have the privilege to read. The following writers are some of the most experienced and well-educated individuals in their fields of philosophy, science, and religion.

In *At the Origins of Christian Worship*, author Larry W. Hurtado writes the following:

> This full cultic reverence which may be described as 'worship' is given to Jesus, not because early Christians

felt at liberty to do so, but because they felt required to do so by God. They reverenced Jesus in observance of God's exaltation of him and in obedience to God's revealed will. This conviction is expressed polemically in John 5:23: that all may honor the Son Just as they honor the Father. Anyone who does not honor the Son does not honor the Father who sent him. (97)

Accordingly, when we Christians properly acclaim Jesus as the one unique Kyrios (Lord), we do so "to the glory of God the Father" (Phil. 2:9–11), and not apart from or in neglect of the glory of the one God and the monotheistic concern reflected in this Pauline phrase. (104)

In *Baker's Dictionary of Theology*, editor Everett F. Harrison writes,

Man is no longer feeling out after God but is resting on the divine self-disclosure in Christ. God has become incarnate in his Son, who confirmed the revelation in the OT and added to it by his teaching and by personal Impact. To see him was to see the Father. The miraculous element In Christianity is agreeable to its supernatural nature. History ceases to be a riddle. Eternity has dipped into time; Divine nature has taken human form in order reveal itself fully and to lift man into fellowship with God. (116)

He is the One who, in uttering what is simply his own mind, at the same time utters the eternal and decisive word of God. (Matt. 5:22–28; 24–35). His word effects what it proclaims (Matt. 8:3; Mark 11:21 as God's word does. He has the authority and power even to forgive sins. Mark 2:1–12. (117)

They prayed to him as they would pray to God (Acts 7:59 f.; I Cor. 1:2; cf. Rev. 9:14, 21; 22: 16). His name as Lord is linked in the closet association with that of

God himself (1 Cor. 1:3; II Cor.1 :2; cf. Rev. 17:14; 19:16; and Deut. 10:17). To him are referred the promises and attributes of the "Lord" God (Kyrios, LXX) in the OT (cf. Acts 2:21 and 38; Rom. 10:3 and Joel 2:32; I Thess. 5:2 and Amos 5:18; Phil 2:10 f., and Isa. 45:23).To him are freely applied the language and formulae which are use of God himself, so that it is difficult to decide in e.g., a passage like Rom. 9;5 whether it is the Father or the Son to whom reference is made. In John 1:1; 1:18; 20:28; II Thess. 1:12; I Tim. 3.16; Tit. 2:13 and II Pet. 1:1. Jesus is confessed as God. (119)

At the Reformation, Luther's Christology was based on Christ as true God and true man in inseparable unity. (121)

The eternal Logos unveiled the absolute image of God by himself assuming the form of man (John 1:14, 18). The doctrine of divine incarnation (q.v.) centrally means that Jesus Christ is the supreme revelation of God, the very image of the invisible Father: "He that hath seen me hath seen the Father". That Jesus of Nazareth is the supreme and express image of God, and not simply a created image, is the clear teaching of Scripture. (278)

At the creation, the Logos was already present ("in the beginning" relates to Gen. 1:1), in the closest relationship with God ... Indeed, "the Logos was God." (327)

The entire work of creation was carried out through the Logos. The source of life and the light of the world and of every man and still continuing this work, the Logos became incarnate, revealing the sign of God's presence and his nature. (327)

John's Logos is not only God's agent in creation; He is God and becomes incarnate, revealing and redeeming. ... The source of John's Logos doctrine is in the person and work of the historical Christ. ... Christ is God's active Word, his saving revelation to fallen man. (328)

Like the liberals, the neo-orthodox are theists. But unlike the liberals, they insist on the transcendence of God. God is in heaven and we on earth. There is, as Kierkegaard would say, an absolute qualitative difference between God and man, therefore man can never discover God at the end of a syllogism. The only way God can be known is by revelation, that is, personal self-disclosure, and this has happened in the person of Jesus Christ. ... In Jesus and in him only, the true God truly speaks to man. (375)

The evidences of Christ's per-eminence are manifold: He alone is the image of the invisible God. He is the pre-existent creator and the perpetual sustainer of the universe, the great Head of creation. He is the triumphant Head of the church, the first conqueror of death. He is the possessor of all fullness-whether of virtue or blessing, especially the blessing of reconciliation to God. (417)

Behold, the tabernacle of God is with men, and he will dwell with them, and they shall be his people, and God himself shell be with them, and be their God. (Rev. 21: 8) (419)

In *Christ the Center*, author George A. F. Knight writes,

It is no accident that God revealed himself in a particular language and a particular culture. The time would come when God took on human being definitively; in Jesus of Nazareth. Now a metaphor like the two-sided coin may help Gentiles to understand the incarnation- but the concept of incarnation, as we shall see, is more than metaphor it is at the heart of how God reveals himself. (7)

The WORD of God, spoken by God, the living God, and proceeding (alive) from the 'heart' of God, is visible and audible performance of the will of God in action in the field of human endeavor. (29)

John's Gospel, consequently, when it seeks to tell us who Jesus is begins at the same place as Genesis 1:1. John 1:1-3 runs "in the beginning was the Word, and the Word was with God (in his 'heart'), and the Word was God." (Note, the Word is no 'thing', but is 'He', on the ground that God is the 'living' God of the Hebrew text of the Old Testament.) "He was in the beginning with God. All things came into being through him … What has come into being in him was life (the life of the living God), and the life was the light of all people." (31)

Philippians (2:6) "Though he was in the form of God." (34)

Here Christ as God is described in very personal terms. (34)

But the whole New Testament proclaims that in Christ we have one full manifestation in the flesh, of God coming to bring about human redemption by building the kingdom around himself on earth as in heaven. (35)

John wishes to emphasize that the Word of God had 'descended' from the realm of the Spirit and had "become, no longer a mental image no longer a philosophical idea, but a human being in history. (37)

So, both Genesis and Daniel contributed to Jesus naming himself Son of Man. His doing so has given us one of the best theological pictures of what we mean when we speak of the Incarnation of the Son of God. "For he is both true human and true God." (42)

J. Gresham Machen, DD, writes in *Christianity and Liberalism,*

> The answer cannot be at all in doubt. The apostle Paul clearly stood always toward Jesus in a truly religious relationship. Jesus was not for Paul merely an example for faith; He was primarily the object of faith. The religion of Paul did not consist in having faith in God like, the faith which Jesus had in God; it consisted rather in having faith in Jesus. (81)

> However, that may be, the term "Lord," which is Paul's regular designation of Jesus, is really just as much a designation of deity as is the term "God." It was a designation of deity even in the pagan religions with which Paul's converts were familiar; and (what is far more important) in the Greek translation of the Old Testament which was current in Paul's day and was used by the Apostle himself, the term was used to translate the; "Jahwe" of the Hebrew text. And Paul does not hesitate to apply to Jesus stupendous passages in the Greek Old Testament where the term Lord thus designates the God of Israel. But what is perhaps most significant of all for the establishment of the Pauline teaching about the Person of Christ is that Paul everywhere stands in a religious attitude toward Jesus. He who is thus the object of religious faith is surely no mere man, but a supernatural Person and indeed a Person who was God. (97)

> The thought of Christ as a super-angelic Being, like God but not God belongs, evidently to pagan mythology and not to the Bible or to Christian faith. It will usually be admitted, if the theistic conception of the separateness between man and God be held, that Christ is either God or else simply man; He is certainly not a being intermediate between God and man. If, then, He is not

merely man, but a supernatural Person, the conclusion is that, He is God. (118)

In the second place, it has already been observed that in the New Testament and in all true Christianity, Jesus is no mere example for faith, but the object of faith. And the faith of which Jesus is the object is clearly religious faith; the Christian man reposes confidence in Jesus in a way that would be out of place in the case or any other than God. (118)

The truth is, the witness of the New Testament is everywhere the same; the New Testament everywhere presents one who was both God and man. (114)

Jesus was God and man in two distinct natures. (115)

The Jesus of the New Testament is "God and man." (115)

In *Early Christian Doctrines*, J. N. D. Kelly writes,

Clement and 'Barnabas' have each special traits of their own. The former opens by advising its readers to 'think of Jesus Christ as of God as the judge of living and dead'. He is our Savior, and "through Him we have known the Father of truth." (91)

[Referring to Ignatius] "Much more frequently, however, he speaks of God the Father and Jesus Christ, declaring that 'there is one God, Who has revealed Himself through His Son Jesus Christ, Who is His Word emerging from silence'. Christ is the Father's 'thought', 'the unlying mouth by which the Father spoke truly'. Ignatius even declares that He is 'our God'; describing Him as 'God incarnate' and 'God made manifest as man'. He was 'in spirit united with the Father'. In His pre-existent being 'ingenerate' (the technical term reserved to distinguish the increate God from creatures), He was the timeless, invisible, impalpable, impassible one who for our sakes entered time and became visible, palpable and passable. His divine Sonship dates from the incarnation. (92)

The Word's otherness, he though, was implied (a) by the alleged appearance of God in the Old Testament (e.g. to Abraham by the oaks of (Mamre), which suggest' that, 'below the Creator of all things, there is Another Who is, and is called, God and Lord', since it is inconceivable that 'the Master and Father of all things should have abandoned all supercelestial affairs and made Himself visible in a minute comer of the world'; (b) by the frequent, Old Testament passages (e.g. Gen. 1, 26: 'Let us make man act.') which represent God as conversing with another, Who is presumably a rational being like Himself; and (c) by the great Wisdom texts, such as Prov. 8.22 ff. ('The Lord created me a beginning of His ways etc.:'), since everyone must agree that the offspring is other than its begetter. So, the Logos, 'having; been put forth as an offspring" from the Father, was with Him before all creatures," and the father had conversed with Him' And He is divine: 'being Word and first-begotten of God, He is also God. 'Thus, then, He is adorable, He is God'; and 'we adore and love, next to God, the Logos derived from the increate and ineffable God, seeing that for our sakes He became man." (97)

The Johannine basis of this theology is apparent, and it finds characteristic expression in such statements as, "The Son reveals the knowledge of the Father through His own manifestation, for the Son's manifestation is the making known of the Father': and, 'What is invisible in the Son is the Father, and what is visible in the Father is the Son. So, in the Old Testament theophanies (here he was in full agreement with Justin) it was really the Word Who spoke with the patriarchs. In the incarnation the Word, hitherto Himself invisible to human eyes, became, visible and disclosed for the first time that image of God in the likeness of which man was originally made. (107)

Naturally the Son is fully divine: 'the father is God, and the Son is God, for whatever is begotten of God is God." (107)

Hippolytus had little difficulty in pointing out to the grand succession of teachers going back to the first century, 'by all of whom Christ is acknowledged as divine' and whose works "proclaim Christ as both God and man." (117)

The vast majority of Christians in the early second century probably shared the faith and practice of the simple Bithynian believers who, as they confessed to Pliny, were in the habit of meeting together before dawn and singing a hymn 'to Christ as to God. (143)

Yet He did not cease to exist as Word, being in fact at once 'God and man'. (Justin) (145)

[Referring to Irenaeus] Only if the divine Word entered fully into human life could the redemption have been accomplished. Similarly, as against Docetism, he argued for the reality of Christ's corporeal nature. He was 'truly God 'and 'truly man.' (148)

Tertullian leaves one in no doubt that it was He, the divine spirit, Who 'took the man to Himself' (suscepit hominem) and mingled God and man in Himself. (151)

He sums up; 'We observe a twofold condition, not confused but conjoined, Jesus in one person at once God and man'. (151)

Novatian, declares that Christ is both God and man. (152)

Clement, The Logos, he states, 'has come to us from heaven'; the Lord has entered into', or 'attached' Himself to human flesh. In becoming incarnate and so making Himself visible, He has begotten Himself, i.e. created His own humanity. So, Christ is human and divine-; alone both, God and man. (154)

(Clement) As God Christ forgives us our sins. (184)

(Origen) He is entitled to be called God. (226)

The following is a translation of the creed which the council drafted and required all the bishops present to sign:
    "We believe in one God, the Father almighty, maker of all things, visible and invisible; And in one Lord Jesus Christ, the Son of God, begotten from the Father, only-begotten, that is, from the substance of the Father, God from God, light from light, true God from true God, begotten not made, of one substance with the Father, through Whom all things came into being, things in heaven and things on earth, Who because of us men and because of our salvation came down and became incarnate, becoming man, suffered and rose again on the third day ascended to the heavens, and will come to judge the living and the dead." (232)

Our immediate task is to investigate the theological attitude of the council, as expressed principally in this creed. From the negative point of view there can be no doubt what that attitude was. Arianism, it is clear, at any rate in its original form outlined in the previous section, was placed under a decisive ban. The Son, the creed state emphatically, is begotten, not made; He is also 'true God', i.e., not God in a secondary degree. Anyone who affirms that the Father pre-existed the Son, or that the Son is a creature produced out of nothingness, or is subject to moral change or development, is formally declared a heretic. In thus repudiating Arianism we may reasonably conjecture that the fathers of Nicaea share Alexander's conviction that Scripture and tradition alike attested the divinity and immutability of the Word. (232–233)

(Athanasius) 'The Son is the Father's image.' (245)

"Hence anyone who sees Christ sees the Father." (245)

"The Son', he argues, 'is of cores other than the Father as offspring, but as God He is one and the same;" (245)

(Gregory) God having become man and man God. (297)

(Gregory of Nyssa) Thus, 'God came to be in human', but the manner of the union is as mysterious and in explicable as the union between body and soul in man. (299)

Cyril thus envisaged the Incarnate as the divine Word living on earth as very man. Here lay the strength of his position from the religious and soteriological standpoints; the Jesus of history was God Himself in human flesh, living and dying and rising again for men. (321)

(Cyril) "Immanuel, he argued, that is, the Lord made flesh, was to be worshipped with a single, indivisible adoration." (322)

(Cyril) "Christ is very God, the Word having become flesh and sharing our flesh and blood ... He is simultaneously God and man." (325)

For Hilary, for example, the two natures of Christ (he regularly uses the term nature) are United in one Person. Christ is true man and true God. (334)

(Augustine) taught that "Christ is one person of twofold substance being both God and man." (336)

The council was transferred to Chalcedon, as being nearer the capital and thus more convenient for Marcion. More than five hundred bishops took part, the Pope as usual being represented by legates; the proceeding opened on 8 October. (451)

In agreement, therefore, with the holy fathers, we all unanimously teach that we should confess that our Lord Jesus Christ is one and the same Son, the same perfect in Godhead and the same perfect in manhood, truly God and truly man, the same of a rational soul and body, consubstantial with the Father in Godhead, and the same consubstantial with us in manhood, like us in all things except sin; begotten from the Father before the ages as regards His Godhead, and in the last days, the same. (339)

Very God as He is. (377)

(Cyril) "It was God incarnate." (385)

(Augustine) "It is through His humanity that Christ exalts us to God and brings God down to us." (391)

(Augustine) "We could never have been delivered by the one mediator ... were He not also God." (391)

In *Evangelism in the Early Church,* Michael Green writes,

> First and foremost is their confidence in the truth of their message. They were all Jews, those first disciples, ardent monotheists. They were the hardest people in the world to convince that God had come to this earth in the person of Jesus to share his life with humankind. (14)

> It would not have been so bad if Christians had contented themselves with asserting that Jesus was the Messiah. But they went much further. The earliest baptismal confession that we can trace is the short assertion that 'Jesus is Lord'. It must be remembered that 'Lord' was the particular name for God in the Old Testament: in the LXX it translates *Adonai.* There could be no mistake about the matter. Jesus himself, followed by the early Christians, made great play with Psalm 110:1 in which David addresses 'my Lord'. This was interpreted as referring to Jesus, who was thus David's' Lord. Is it any wonder that the Jews thought Christians were preaching a second God? How could they, in their pure monotheism, have any truck with such blasphemy. (53)

> Second, he stressed the final and absolute nature of the gospel; it is the gospel of truth, of hope, of power, of immortality, of the glory of God immanent within our world. It is, in short, the mystery of God, the truth once hid and now revealed to men and women, nothing less than the Wisdom of God.? (86)

> Now this language has obvious affinities with New Testament. It may well be that St Mark is deliberately contrasting the good news with its imperial counterpart in Rome. Both speak salvation, but the Christian is far more profound than the imperial: it embraces rescue

from sin and death as well as political liberation. Both speak the good news of a ruler born, come of age, enthroned: but the Christian *euaggelion* is far more profound than the Imperial: her ruler sits on the throne of the universe, not merely of the Empire and his birth is a real incarnation of the only God, not the mock deity of the Imperial dynasty. (87)

2 Samuel 7: The New Age dawn with the resurrection, the accession of Jesus to the Lordship of the universe.' The 'Hellenistic creed said: 'In Jesus Christ God has encountered the world not casually but definitely and finally. The dominance of the law and of the forces of evil has been overthrown through the Son of God. (96)

All Christians were convinced that Jesus Christ was God's last word to mankind, the one who brought as much of God to us as we could appreciate in the only terms we could take it in, the terms of a human life; the one who in dying and rising again was manifestly vindicated in his claims and achievement. This they all believed in common: (96)

John is convinced, what has happened. The Absolute became our Contemporary: God became man for thirty years or so in order to bring us to a new dimension of life through knowing him. (111)

The deity of Jesus is fundamental; he is Truth, the Light of the world, the Word of God who is himself God. (113)

Here were Christian Jews applying to a crucified Rabbi the word 'Lord' which had been used in the Old Testament as the most frequent title for Yahweh's ineffable name. (141)

Passages which in the Old Testament refer to Yahweh are unashamedly applied to Jesus in the New. (146)

His whole significance depended on his being the manifestation of the one true God. (181)

How does a person come to Christianity? It is through faith alone that God can be known, a faith that brings joy, love and the desire to imitate Christ. 'No man has either seen him or made him known, but he has revealed himself. And he has " … manifested himself through faith, by which alone it is given to behold God." (191)

(Macarius) "Let us then welcome the Lord our God." (194)

(Clement) "Believe him who is man and God." (297)

Genesis in Space and Time author Francis A. Schaeffer writes,

In the beginning already was [the Greek imperfect here is better translated *already was* then was] the Word and the Word already was with God and the Word already was God. The same was in the beginning with God. (22)

Revelation 4:11 contains a great doxology to this One. Unfortunately, the King James translation does not give its full force. The first phrase should read: "Worthy art thou, our Lord and our God." This reminds us of Jeremiah's phrase, "He is our portion." He is our Lord and our God. Then the verse continues: "Worthy art thou, our Lord and our God, to receive the glory and the honor and the power: for thou didst create all things, and because of thy will they were, and were created" (ASV). The New English Bible correctly translates it in modem terms: "By thy will they were created, and have their being!" This Is the Christian cosmogonie. (25)

God in Three Persons author Millard J. Erickson writes,

> Summarized by Kelly: "Reduced to their simplest, these were the convictions that God had made Himself known in the Person of Jesus the Messiah, raising Him from the dead and offering salvation to men through Him, and that He had poured out His Holy Spirit upon the Church." There was a strong belief in the special status of Jesus Christ. He was the one in whom (or through whom) they had salvation. He had more fully revealed the truth of God than had any of the prophets. And he was to be worshiped, just as the Jews had worshiped Jehovah." (34)

> The second letter of Clement to the Corinthians is actually a sermon rather than an epistle. It is, indeed, the oldest surviving sermon of the Christian church after the New Testament. It begins with the exhortation: "Brethren, we ought so to think of Jesus Christ as of God, as of the judge of living and dead. (38)

> Ignatius's references to issues related to the Trinity are more extensive. Most of his statements are dyadic in nature. He says that "there is one God, who has revealed Himself through His Son Jesus Christ, Who is His Word emerging from silence. He speaks of Christ as "the Invisible, who for our sake became visible." (39)

> He describes him as the Father's "thought." He even refers to him as "our God" and describes him as "God incarnate" and "God manifested" as man. (39)

> Thus, in Luke 11:20, Jesus is reported as saying, "But if I drive out demons by the finger of God, then the kingdom of God has come to you." In Matthew 12:28, however, Matthew reports the words of Jesus as being, "But if I drive out demons by the Spirit of God, then the

kingdom of God has come upon you." Irenaeus makes clear that the Son is fully divine: "the Father is God, and the Son is God, for whatever is begotten of God is God." (50)

There is also the famous statement: "What is invisible in the Son is the Father, and what is visible in the Father is the Son." The parallelism between the Word and Wisdom, the Son and the Spirit, certainly seems to establish the divinity of the Spirit as well. Irenaeus says that we "should know that He who made, and formed … and nourishes us by means of the creation, establishing all things by His Word, and binding them together by His Wisdom—this is He who is the only true God." (14)

Basil put it this way: "Everything that the Father is, is seen in the "Son, and everything that the Son is, belongs to the Father. The Son in His entirety abides in the Father and in return possess the Father in entirety in Himself. Thus, the hypostasis of the Son is, so to speak, the form and presentation by which the Father is known, and the Father's hypostasis is recognized in the form the Son." (92)

Richardson says that this concept of a relation between God and a supramundane being involves the idea that God works through agents, which are angelic beings. In the case of Jesus, the relation involves more than that. "It means, "he says, "that the Word or Son is that aspect or 'mode of being' of God whereby he comes into relationship with the world, whereby he creates and reveals himself." (101)

"It follows from this that Christianity, and Christianity alone, was founded by God in person on the only occasion on which he has ever become incarnate in this world, so that Christianity has a unique status as the way of salvation provided and appointed by God himself." (151)

The final Pauline reference is in Titus 3:4-6, although of course some would not consider this, or any of the pastoral epistles, to be of Pauline authorship. Paul writes that, when the kindness and love of "God our Savior" appeared (v. 4), he saved us through the "washing of rebirth and renewal by the Holy Spirit" (v. 5), whom he "poured out on us generously through Jesus Christ our Savior" (v. 6). All of the persons of the Trinity are actively involved in salvation, each in his own respective fashion. (188)

He [Paul] then goes beyond those passages, saying, "yet for us there is but one God, the Father, from whom all things came and for whom we live; and there is but one Lord, Jesus Christ, through whom all things came and through whom we live." Other texts also give clear indication that the Son had a major role in creation. John 1:3 says, "Through him all things were made; without him nothing was made that has been made." The writer to Hebrews cites God as saying to the Son, "In the beginning, O Lord, you laid the foundations of the earth, and the heavens are the work of your hands." (235–236)

An immanent theology of God is therefore simply a summary of the one revelation of God to us in Jesus Christ. (297)

While he refers to the one person as "God," the use of the term "Lord" would, for Paul who had been reared as a strict Jew, be virtually an equivalent for "God." He was Paul's Lord, and was really his favorite name for Jesus. (300)

We may begin by noting that very early, even during the New Testament times, Christians worshiped Jesus. Much quoted is the early statement of the younger Pliny. Writing to Emperor Trajan in A.D. 112, he reported that the Christians sang hymns to their Lord "as God." Examples of these hymns have been preserved for us in the New Testament. There is wide scholarly agreement, for example, that Philippians 2:6–11 and Colossians 1:15–20 were not merely passages written by Paul, but were existing hymns used within the church that Paul incorporated into his writings. In Philippians 2:10–11 Paul quotes from Isaiah 45:23, where Yahweh declares his own uniqueness as Lord. In other words, this was seen as a continuation of the Old Testament worship of Yahweh. (315)

There are, however, some other, clearer instances of worship of Jesus in the Gospels. The most definite is Thomas's "My Lord and my God" in John 20:28. Less obvious is Peter's expression in Luke 5:8, "Go away from me, Lord; I am a sinful man!" This was the story of the miraculous catch of fish, obtained under unfavorable conditions (in daylight and in the deep part of the lake, after they had fished unsuccessfully all night). Peter's falling at Jesus' feet, his confession of his sinfulness, and his use of "Lord" suggest that he was aware of Jesus' deity and was paying homage to him. (317)

One of the most significant instances of such expression: found in Romans 10:13: "Everyone who calls on the name of the Lord will be saved," a quotation from Joel 2:32. That Paul is here referring to Jesus seems evident from verse 9, where he says that if one confesses with one's mouth,

"Jesus is Lord," one will be saved. Calling on the Lord is evidently asking Jesus for salvation. The reception of Christ as Savior and committing oneself to him as Lord is an act of prayer. Becoming a Christian is essentially a direct response to Christ. He says in Revelation 3:20, "Here I am! I stand at the door and knock. If anyone hears my voice and opens the door, I will go in and eat with him, and he with me." Persons do not become Christians by praying to Father, asking him to apply the redeeming work of Christ to their lives. Rather, they come to the Father through the Son (John 14:6). (320)

In *How Should We Then Live? The Rise and Decline of Western Thought and Culture*, author Francis A. Schaeffer, speaking about the Christians in Rome, writes,

> We may express the nature of their rebellion in two ways, both of which are true. First, we can say they worshiped Jesus as God and they worshiped the infinite-personal God only. Caesars would not tolerate this worshiping of the one God *only*. It was counted as treason. Thus, their worship became a special threat to the unity of the state during the third century and during the reign of Diocletian (284–305). (24)

In *Introduction to Religious Philosophy*, Geddes MacGregor writes,

> Christianity is a religion whose doctrine, in its historic, orthodox form, is a special form of theism, extremely rich and complex. For Christians hold that God penetrated His own creation in a unique way, by taking human flesh in the person of Jesus Christ, in whom, therefore, God may be seen perfectly revealed to us in terms of our own human nature. Nevertheless, although Christ makes human salvation possible, the golf between God and man is preserved: even in

heaven, where man's individuality is perfectly and fully developed, man never becomes God. That man should become "as God" was Satan's deceitful promise, a means of tempting man to indulge in delusions of self-grandeur that would be his undoing, leading him to misery and ruin. So Christian doctrine, by its elaborate provisions, expresses to the fullest extent both the remoteness and inaccessibility of God, on the one hand, and on the other, His intimate nearness and abiding presence. In Christianity, theism is presented in its most startling, provocative and dramatic form. (82–83)

Is the Holy Spirit for Me? author, Harvey Floyd, writes,

> The force of John's statement is: "the word was Deity;" "Christ possessed the full nature and qualities of God." (9)

> In his deity, he always knew; as God, he was omniscient. In his humanity he had to learn, and, in his humanity, there were things he did not know. He did not know the time of his second coming (Matt. 24:36). In his Godhood he knew; in his manhood he did not. (9)

> Paul says: "In him dwells all the fullness of Godhood bodily." He is fully or completely God. All the qualities and attributes that make God God, he possesses." (9)

> And the Word was God, "He possessed all the fullness of God-hood (Col. 2:9). That is contrary to Arianism. He was not a lesser god; he was God, All the attributes and qualities which God the Father possessed, he possessed. He was truly God, and yet he was different in his person from God the Father. So, what we have is truly one God, but we do not have a simplistic unity. What we have is the doctrine of the Trinity: that God is a triad, that God is one God indeed, but his unity is a complex unity, a

unity that exists in diversity. If it is true that God exists in three persons, then John 1:1 is intelligible. (13)

Does "begotten" mean that Christ was brought into existence, that he is not eternal, and that he is inferior to the Father, as Arius maintained? Look at the context which surrounds the statement ("I have begotten thee") in Hebrews. In verse three Christ is declared to be the-exact representation of God's nature ("the very image of his substance"). How can he exactly represent God's nature if he is a creature and is inferior in his nature? Hebrews 1:6 says: "Let all the angels of God worship him." Jesus maintained that God alone is the true object of worship (Matt. 4:10, quoting Dt. 6:13). Peter rejected the worship of Cornelius (Acts 10:25, 26). The angel corrected John when he fell before him to worship (Rev. 19:10, 22:9). Yet Jesus permitted himself to be worshipped (Matt. 28:9, 17). He did not correct Thomas when the apostle called him "my Lord and my God" (John 20:28). According to Hebrews, further, Christ is addressed as God by the Father (1:8), is Creator (1: 10), and is eternal and unchanging (1: 12), a sure attribute of God (Ps. 90:2). In Acts 13:33 Paul interpreted the begetting of Christ as referring, not to a beginning in time, but to the resurrection-that is, Christ was "begotten" when God officially declared him to be the Messiah and invested him as Messiah in the resurrection." (15–16)

In *Jesus and Christian Origins Outside the New Testament*, F. F. Bruce writes,

But they maintained that their fault or error amounted to nothing more than this: they were in thy habit of meeting on a certain fixed day before sunrise and reciting an antiphonal hymn to Christ as God. (26)

For one who is dead cannot rise of his own accord (though he may do so when helped by the prayer of another righteous man), unless he is an angel or another of the heavenly powers, or unless God himself appears as a man and accomplishes what he wills, and walks with men and falls and lies down and rises again, as he so pleases. (52)

Jesus truly rose, for in him God appeared on earth as a man. (52)

Murray J. Harris writes in *Jesus as God—The New Testament Use of Theos in Reference to God*,

And in the spurious fourth Oration against the Arians, Pseudo Athanasius inveighs principally against the Marcellians in a treatise that begins "the Word is God from God and closes "so then he himself is God the word. So, Christ is the God-man, born of Mary. (9)

No one who turns from reading a church father such as Ignatius back to the NT can help being impressed by the remarkable reserve of the N T writers in applying the term (*GOD) to Jesus. Nowhere in the Gospels or Epistles or the Apocalypse does one expressions such as those of Ignatius: "for our God, Jesus the CHRIST was conceived by Mary" (Eph. 18:2); "love for Jesus Christ, our God" "permit me to be an imitator of the passion of my God"(Rom. 6:3); "I give glory to Jesus Christ, the God who granted you such wisdom" (Smyr. 1:1). (9)

The questions that arise jostle for attention. Does the NT ever parallel the boldness of Ignatius in designating Jesus as (*God)? If the writers of the NT were persuaded of the deity of Christ, what accounts for their reticence to ascribe to him the title that, of all the divine names, would seem most explicitly to affirm that deity? Have the fathers and the creeds of the church outstripped the NT evidence in speaking so plainly and so often of Jesus Christ as "God"? (9-10)

Those who clearly perceived, through the visible creation, that God exists and that he possesses "eternal power and deity" ("they knew God,") are without excuse for they failed to give him the glory that is his due because of who he is "they did not honor him as God." (39)

Inasmuch as the only Son is God by nature and intimately acquainted with the Father by experience he is uniquely qualified to reveal the nature and character of God. (102)

Thomas said to him, "My Lord and my God!" (John 20:28). (110)

It was precisely because Jesus was believed to be *universally* Lord and God that John was motivated to write and carefully placed this significant devotional cry at the end of his Gospel as the point of confession to which he wished to lead his readers. (122)

But more is implied than mere representation. Thomas was addressing Jesus as one who shared Yahweh's authority and functions an exercised Yahweh's rights. It was a case of (c. John 20:21). Jesus deserved human Worship as the one in whom was vested the ultimate authority to forgive sin (John 20:23; cf.). Mark 2:5–10), the one who dispensed the Holy Spirit to his followers (John 20:22) and commissioned them to divine service (John 20:21), the one who by virtue of his resurrection possessed "the keys that unlock death and Hades" (Rev. 1: 18 Moffatt), and the one who was to climax his resurrection by ascension to the Father (John 20:17). (123)

The Gospel was written to produce belief that Jesus was the promised Jewish Messiah and that this Messiah was none other than the "one and only" Son of God who had come from the Father (John 11:42; 17:8), who shared his nature (John 1:1. 18; 10:30) and fellowship (John 1:18; 14:11), and who therefore might appropriately be addressed and worshiped as (GOD).*, (The writer uses the Greek term), Unique sonship implies deity (John 5:18; cf. 19:7). (125)

From this viewpoint, John 20:28 represents an advance on John 1:1. Jesus not only was already at the beginning of creation John 1:1. At the time when Thomas spoke, and John wrote, it could be said (by implication), "Jesus *is* Lord and God." (126)

We move from (1:1) to (1:18) to (20:28); from Jesus Christ as a participant in the divine essence to his being "the only Son, who fully shares the Divine nature to his being the God who is worshiped by believers; from the preexistent Logos who eternally enjoyed active communion with the Father to the incarnate Son who always resides in the Father's heart and on earth revealed him (1:18) to the resurrected Lord who may be rightfully hailed by his devotee as "my God." (128)

John, Jesus is appropriately designated (God)*, writer uses the Greek), his preexistent, incarnate, and post-resurrection states. Of all the titles used of Jesus in the Fourth Gospel God, * would therefore seem to represent the culmination. (129)

One week after his resurrection, and because of a resurrection appearance, Jesus was adoringly addressed by Thomas with the exclamation, "My Lord and My God!," a confessional invocation that not only marks the climax (along with the accompanying beatitude) of the Thomas periscope, and John 20, but also forms the culmination of the entire Gospel. Just as Israel had honored Yahweh as (e.g., Ps 98:8 LXX and Christians honored the Father as *, The Lord of me and the God of me, (the writer uses the Greek) (Rev. 4:11), so now people were to "honor the Son, even as they honor the Father" (John 5:23), by addressing him with the words, *the Lord of me and the God of me. In uttering this confessional cry Thomas recognized the lordship of Jesus in 'the physical and spiritual realms as well as over his own life (*the Lord of me) and the essential oneness of Jesus with the Father which made his worship of Jesus legitimate (* the God of me). As used in this verse, *Lord; and God are titles, not proper names, the first implying and the second explicitly affirming the substantial deity of the risen Jesus. (129)

This review of each phrase in Romans 9:5b has shown that it is exegetically more satisfactory to apply the second part of the verse to Christ then to God the Father. And it has shown that the immediate context supports such a conclusion. If this is so, it follows that at least two distinct affirmations are made regarding Christ; he is "over all and blessed forever." (165)

In Romans 9:5b one may isolate three distinct affirmations about Christ: he is Lord of all, he is God by nature, and he will be eternally praised. (167)

The majority of post-Nicene writers support the identification of (the great God and Savior of us) * (the author uses the Greek) as Christ." (185)

In the light of the foregoing evidence, it seems highly probable that in Titus 2:13 Jesus is Christ called "our great God and savior," a verdict shared, with varying degrees of assurance, by almost all grammarians, and lexicographer many commentators, and many NT theolog Christology, although there are some dissenting voices. (185)

(Using the book of Hebrews he writes)

Jesus is described as the perfect representation of God's glory and nature (1:3); he not only existed before he appeared on earth (10:5), before Melchizedek (7:3), before human history began (1:2), or before the universe was created (1:10), but he also existed and exists eternally (7:16; 9:14; 13:8); like his Father he may be called "Lord"; he is creator (1:10), sustainer,(1:3), and heir (1:2) of the universe, that is, everything in time and space (1:2); he is "Son" and "the Son of God" the timeless of (1:3) pointing to a natural, not adoptive, sonship; he is worshiped by angels (1:6) and is the object of human faith (12:2); he is sovereign over the world to come (2:5); and passages referring to Yahweh in the OT are applied to him. (225)

From the detailed exegetical analysis in chapters ll-XII, I conclude that it is certain that the term (God)*(the author uses the Greek) is applied to Jesus Christ in John 1:1 and John 20:28, very probable in Romans 9:5, Titus 2:13, Hebrews 1:8, and 2 Peter 1:1, and probable John 1:18, an possible but not likely in Acts 20:28, Hebrews 1:9, and 1 John 5:20 (see table 5). Other passages to which appeal is sometimes made include Matthew 1:23, John 17:3, Galatians 2:20, Ephesians 5:5, Colossians 2:2, 2 Thessalonians 1:12, and 1 Timothy 3:16. In none of these latter verses is a christological use of (God)*(the author uses the Greek) at all likely. In subsequent discussion in this chapter I shell therefore assume that (God)*(the author uses the Greek) is applied to Jesus in seven NT passages: John 1:1, John 1:18; John 20:28, Romans 9:5, Titus, 2:13 Hebrews 1:8, and 2 Peter 1:1. (271)

According to Dunn, so, in Christianity Christ as Sophia-Logos incarnate was understood not as being distinct from God but as the clearest expression of the presence of God himself. "Christ is divine in no other sense than as God immanent, God himself acting to redeem as he did to create." (280)

An Outline of the New Testament Testimony to the Deity of Christ (315–317)

This outline does not purport to be in any sense an exhaustive analysis of the NT witness to Christ's deity. Rather it is a sketch of one approach a rather traditional approach-to this theme. Other complementary or supplementary approaches abound, such as the creative treatment of Jesus' implicit claim to deity in his parables by P. B. Payan or R.T. France's documentation from the Synoptic Gospels of Jesus' assumption of the role of Yahweh (Jesus 150–59). For a brief discussion of the NT verses that seem, at first sight, to call Jesus' divinity into question, see R. E. Brown, Reflections 6–10 (= "Jesus"). (548–51)

A. Implicit Christology
  1. Divine functions performed by Jesus
    a. In relation to the universe
    Creator (John 1:3; Col. 1:16; Heb. 1:2)
    Sustainer (1 Cor. 8:6; Col. 1:17; Heb. 1:3)
    Author of life (John 1:4; Acts 3:15) (4) Ruler (Matt. 28:18; Rom. 14:9; Rev. 1:5)
    b. In relation to human beings
    Healing the sick (Mark 1:32–34; Acts 3:6; 10:38)
    Teaching authoritatively (Mark 1:21–22; 13:31)

Forgiving sins (Mark 2:1–12; Luke 24:47; Acts 5:31; Col. 3:13)

Granting salvation or imparting eternal life (Acts 4:12; Rom. 10:12–14)

Dispensing the Spirit (Matt. 3:11; Acts 2:17, 33)

Raising the dead (Luke 7:11–17; John 5:21; 6:40)

Exercising judgment (Matt. 25:31–46; John 5:19–29; Acts 10:42; 1 Cor. 4:4–5) 2. Divine status claimed by or accorded to Jesus

a. In relation to his Father

Possessor of divine attributes (John 1:4; 10:30; 21:17; Eph. 4:10; Col. 1:19; 2:9)

Eternally existent (John 1:1; 8:58; 12:41; 17:5; 1 Cor. 10:4; Phil. 2:6; Heb. 11:26; 13:8; Jude 5)

Equal in dignity (Matt. 28:19; John 5:23; 2 Cor. 13:14; Rev. 22:13; cf. 21:6)

Perfect revealer (John 1:18; 14:9; Col. 1:15; Heb. 1:1–3)

Embodiment of truth (John 1:9, 14; 6:32; 14:6; Rev. 3:7, 14)

Joint possessor of the kingdom (Eph, 5:5; Rev. 11:15), churches (Rom. 16:16), Spirit (Rom. 8:9; Phil. 1:19), temple (Rev. 21:22), divine name (Matt 28:19; cf. Rev. 14:1), and throne (Rev. 22:1, 3) b. In relation to human beings

(1) Recipient of praise (Matt. 21:15–16; Eph. 5:19; 1 Tim. 1:12; Rev. 5:8–14)

2) Recipient of prayer (Acts 1:24; 7:59-60; 9:10–17, 21; 22:16,19; 1 Cor. 1:2; 16:22; 2 Cor. 12:8)

(3) Object of saving faith (John 14:1; Acts 10:43; 16:31; Rom. 10:8–13)

4) Object of worship (Matt. 14:33; 28:9, 17; John 5:23; 20:28; Phil, 2:10–11; Heb. 1:6; Rev. 5:8–12)

Joint source of blessing (1 Cor. 1:3; 2 Cor. 1:2; Gal. 1:3; 1 Thess. 3:11; 2 Thess. 2:16)

Object of doxologies (2 Tim. 4:18; 2 Pet. 3:18; Rev. 1:5b–6; 5:13)

B. Explicit Christology
    1. Old Testament passages referring to Yahweh applied to Jesus
    Character of Yahweh (Exod. 3:14 and Isa. 43:11 alluded to in John 8:58; Ps. 101:27–28 LXX [MT 102:28–29] quoted in Heb. 1:11–12; Isa. 44:6 alluded to in Rev. 1:17)
    Holiness of Yahweh (Isa. 8:12–13 [cf. 29:23] quoted in 1 Pet. 3:14–15)
    Descriptions of Yahweh (Ezek. 43:2 and Dan. 10:5–6 alluded to in Rev. 1:1:3–10)
    Worship of Yahweh (Isa. 45:23 alluded to in Phil. 2:10–11; Deut. 32:43 LXX and Ps. 96:7 LXX [MT 97:7] quoted in Heb. 1:6)
    Work of Yahweh in creation (Ps. 101:26 LXX [MT 102:27] quoted in Heb. 1:10)
    Salvation of Yahweh (Joel 2:32 [MT 3:5] quoted in Rom. 10:13; cf.
    Acts 2:21; Isa. 40:3 quoted in Matt. 3:3)
    Trustworthiness of Yahweh (Isa, 28:16 quoted in Rom. 9:33; 10:11; 1 Pet. 2:6)
    Judgment of Yahweh (Isa. 6:10 alluded to in John 12:41; Isa. 8:14 quoted in Rom. 9:33 and 1 Pet. 2:8)
    I. Triumph of Yahweh (Ps. 68:18 [MT v. 19] quoted in Eph. 4:8)
    2. Divine titles claimed by or applied to Jesus
    Son of Man (Matt. 16:28; 24:30; Mark 8:38; 14:62–64; Acts 7:56)
    Son of God (Matt. 11:27; Mark 15:39; John 1:18; Rom. 1:4; Gal. 4:4; Heb. 1:2)
    Messiah (Matt. 16:16; Mark 14:61; John 20:31)
    Lord (Mark 12:35-37; John 20:28; Rom. 10:9; 1 Cor. 8:5–6; 12:3; 16:22; Phil. 2:11; 1 Pet. 2:3; 3:15)

Alpha and Omega (Rev. 22: 13; cf. 1:8; 21:6, of the Lord God)

God (John 1:1. 18; 20:28: Rom. 9:5; Titus 2:13; Heb. 1:8; 2 Pet. 1:1)

(315–317)

Philosophy of Religion author, Norman L Geisler, writes,

But according to biblical theism, God has manifested Himself in human history (the incarnation of Christ) and He did do something to defeat evil (the atonement of Christ) and He did provide assurance—historically verifiable assurance—that this is true, (the resurrection of Christ). (369)

In *Reasonable Faith Christian Truth and Apologetics*, William Lane Craig writes,

Then appeal was made to the eyewitness testimony Of Jesus to show specifically that God had revealed himself in Jesus Christ (Acts 17:30–31:1; Cor. 15:3–8). (22)

Many of the early Christians such as Polycarp, Irenaeus, Athenagoras, Origen, Tertullian, Clement of Alexandria, and so forth were raised in other religions, yet came to worship this man Jesus as God, because they had made a diligent inquiry and discovered that he wrought many miraculous deeds. (213)

Undoubtedly, one of the major stumbling blocks to becoming a Christian for many people today is that Christianity is a religion of miracles. It asserts that God became incarnate in Jesus of Nazareth, being born of a virgin, that he performed various miracles, exorcised demonic beings, and that, having died by crucifixion, he rose from the dead. But the problem is that these sorts of miraculous even seem to belong to a worldview foreign to modern man—a pre-scientific, superstitious worldview belonging to the ancient and middle ages. (247)

These conclusions play havoc with the popular apologetic for Christian based on the claims of Christ. According to popular apologetic, Jesus claimed to be God, and his claims were either true or falsely. If they were false, then either he was intentionally lying or else he deluded. But neither of these alternatives is plausible. Therefore, his claims cannot be false; he must be who he claimed to be, God incarnate, and we must decide whether we shall give our lives to him or not. (299)

The Christological Titles:

Those who deny that Jesus made any personal claims implying divinity face the very severe problem of explaining how it is that the worship of Jesus as Lord and God came about at all in the early church. It does little good to say that the early church wrote its beliefs about Jesus back into the Gospels, for the problem is the very origin of those beliefs themselves. Studies by New Testament scholars such as Larry Hurtado of the University of Edinburgh, Martin Hengel of Tubingen University, C. F. D. Moule of Cambridge, and others have proved that within twenty years of the crucifixion a full blown Christology proclaiming Jesus as God incarnate existed. How does one explain this worship by monotheistic Jews of one of their countrymen whom they had accompanied during his lifetime, apart from the claims of Jesus himself? The great church historian Jaroslav Pelikan points out that all the early Christians shared the conviction that salvation was the work of a being no less than Lord of heaven and earth and that the redeemer was God himself. He observes that the oldest Christian sermon, the oldest account of Christian martyr, the oldest pagan report of the church, and the oldest liturgical prayer (1 Cor. 16:22) all refer to as Lord and God. He concludes," clearly it was the message of what the church believed and taught that 'God' was an appropriate name for Jesus Christ." But if Jesus never made any such claims, then the belief of the earliest Christians in this regard becomes inexplicable. (300)

But even more exalted images of the Messiah existed. Isaiah declared, For to us a child is born, to us a son is given; and the government will be upon his shoulder, and his name will be called "Wonderful Counselor, Mighty God, Everlasting Father, Prince to Peace." Of the increase of his government and of peace there will be no end, upon the throne of David, and over his kingdom, to establish it, and to uphold it with justice and with righteousness from this time forth and for evermore. (Isa. 9:6–7)

Here the Davidic king is called "Mighty God," and his reign is said to endure forever, motifs which are echoed in the *Psalm of Solomon*. Again, in the first-century *Similitude of Enoch* we are presented with "the Lord of the Spirits and his Messiah," who is also called "that Son of Man." (301)

In Jesus' case the proclamation of John the Baptist, that after him would come one mightier than him who would baptize with the Holy Spirit, is seen as the fulfillment of Malachi 3:1 (Rsv): "Behold, I send my messenger to prepare the way for me, and the Lord whom you seek will suddenly come to his temple" and Isaiah 40:3 (esv): "A voice cries, 'In the wilderness prepare the way of the Lord, make straight in the desert a highway for our God." Notice that, according to these prophecies, it is *the Lord himself* who is coming (cf. Isa. 40:5,9-11). The relevant question to be posed here is not whom John expected, but, as the person coming in self-conscious fulfillment of John's predictions, who Jesus took himself to be. It is intriguing that in the Q saying by Jesus on the person of John the Baptist (Matt. 11:10; Luke 7: 27), Jesus himself identifies John as the messenger of Malachi 3:1. In the same discourse Jesus goes on to speak of himself as the Son of Man who has come after John (Matt.11:19; Luke 7:34). Such a divine-human figure would sensibly fulfill the divine and human facets of John's prediction. (310)

This saying has been characterized as a bolt out of the Johannine blue. For what does it tell us about Jesus' self-concept? It tells us that he thought of himself as the exclusive Son of God and the only revelation of God the Father to mankind! It is said by those who deny the saying's authenticity that the unrestricted authority and absoluteness and exclusivity of the postulated relation between the Father and the Son is unparalleled in the pre-Easter Synoptic tradition. But that assumes, implausibly, that passages like Mark 1:11.27 3:11; Matthew 7:21, and so forth, are not part of the per-Easter tradition, for they certainly do contemplate Jesus as the absolute, authoritative Son of God and revealer of the Father.

As Denaux has rightly emphasized, what we have here is a Johannine Christological affirmation in the earliest stratum of the Gospel traditions, an affirmation which forms a bridge to the high Christology of John's Gospel and yet, in light of passages like Mark 4:10–12; 12:1–11; 13:32; and Matthew 16:17–19; 28:18, is also at home in the Synoptic tradition. On the basis of this saying, we may conclude that Jesus thought of himself as God's Son in an absolute and unique sense and as having been invested with the exclusive authority to reveal his Father to men. (312)

Michael F. Lawlor

There is something of a scholarly consensus, as we shall see, that Jesus had a sense of unsurpassed authority. He put himself in God's place by his words and action. (317)

Given the supremely authoritative status of the divinely revealed Torah, Jesus' teaching can only appear presumptuous and even blasphemous. In effect, as Robert Hutchinson put it, Neusner wants to ask Jesus, "Who do you think you are God?" Neusner himself recognizes that "no one can encounter Matthew's Jesus without concurring that before us in the evangelist's mind is God incarnate." But if Jesus' opposition of his personal teaching to the Torah is an authentic facet of the historical Jesus—as even the skeptical scholars of the Jesus Seminar concede—then it seems that Jesus did arrogate to himself the authority of God. (321)

"But if it is by the finger of God that I cast out demons, then the kingdom of God has come upon you" (Luke 11: 20.). This saying, which is recognized by New Testament scholarship as authentic, is remarkable for two reasons. First, it shows that Jesus claimed divine authority over the spiritual forces of evil Second it shows that Jesus believed that in him the kingdom of God had come. In claiming that in him the kingdom of God had already arrived, as visibly demonstrated by his exorcisms, Jesus was, in effect, saying that in himself God had drawn near, thus putting himself in God's place." (322)

The problem is that no one but God had the authority to make such a proclamation, no mere prophet could presume to speak for God on this matter. As Royce Gruenler puts it, Jesus "is consciously speaking as the voice of God on the matters that belong only to God. The evidence clearly leads us to affirm that Jesus implicitly claims to do what only God can do, to forgive sins." (322)

Jesus in effect takes God's place as leader of Israel. (325)

Jesus assumes the place reserved for God in the Old Testament ('So his claim to perform miracles is not only amazing in itself, but actually has a deeper significance in implying Jesus' divinity. (325)

Although we have not discussed all these matters, enough has been said, I think, to indicate the radical self-concept of' Jesus, Here is a man who thought of himself as the promised Messiah, God's only Son, the Danielic Son of man to whom all dominion and authority would be given, who claimed to act and speak with divine authority, who held himself to be a worker of miracles, and who believed that people's eternal destiny hinged on whether or not they believed in him. Gruenler sums it up; "It is a striking fact of modern New Testament research that the essential clues for correctly reading the implicit Christological self-understanding of Jesus are abundantly clear." There is, he concludes, "absolutely convincing" that Jesus did intend to stand in the very place of God himself. (326)

This unheard of claim to authority, as it comes to expression in the antitheses of the Sermon on the Mount, for example, is implicit Christology, since it presupposes a unity of Jesus with God that is deeper than that of all men, namely a unity of essence. This ... claim to authority is explicable only from the side of his deity. This authority only God himself can claim. With regard to Jesus there are only two possible modes of behavior: either to believe that in him God encounters us or to nail him to the cross as a blasphemer. *Tertium non datur.* (327)

The Church at the End of the 20ᵗʰ Century author, Francis A. Schaeffer, writes,

> By contrast, of course, there is the magnificent account in the Bible of Jesus Christ in front of the tomb of Lazarus. Jesus who is God, and claims to be God in the full Trinitarian sense, stands, in front of the tomb, and He is angry. The Greek makes that plain. As Jesus stands there in His anger, we should notice something. The Christ who claims to be God can be angry at the result of the fall and the abnormal event which He now faces *without being angry at Himself.* (29)

The Evangelization of the Roman Empire author, E. Glenn Hinson, writes,

> Christianity brooked no competitors, even the Jews, and the resultant sense of divine mission for the one true God revealed in Jesus Christ compelled Christians to enlist all and sundry in the one true religion. The evangelical fervor of early missionaries like Paul both amused and astounded their contemporaries, accustomed to the broadest type of religious toleration. (29)

> As evolved over the first four or five centuries, the complex system of incorporation into the church involved five relatively distinct phases, each of which was treated with some flexibility according to time and circumstances. What emerges from a study of scores of references is that the whole institution was employed in helping converts to center their allegiance on the one God who had manifested Himself in Jesus Christ and to rise to at least a minimal level of sanctity with a view to bearing witness to him. (74)

Irenaeus, as H. Chadwick has pointed out, propounded a theory of progressive education of the human race. One and the same God revealed himself in both, Testaments through the eternal Logos. (152)

As a rule, for reasons stated earlier, Christian apologists appealed simply for conversion to the worship of the one true God who had revealed himself in the incarnate Logos or Spirit. (229)

Claims of divinity, since they posed a threat to a monotheistic faith, erected the biggest stumbling block to Jewish conversions. The apologists replied from two directions. (1) They assembled texts which would confirm the divinity of the expected Messiah or the incarnation of God. First, they established from Old Testament text how God had dwelled intimately among men (Ps. 83:8; Zech, 9:9; Isa. 65' 1,).

He made his "temple" among men and addressed Israel as "my son" (Hos. 11:1–2; Isa. 1:2; Deut. 14: 1–4). Next, they cited those specific messianic texts which Implied that the Messiah would be God himself (Pss. 2: 7, 110:3; lsa. 7:14; 9:6–7) and found proof that he had already come in passages which stated that the Gentiles would have their hopes fulfilled in him (Gen. 49: 10). Further, they proved his divinity by identifying him with various "types": the Word of God (Gen. 1:1ff.; Pss. 36:2, 44:2; 106:20; Isa. 10:23), the Wisdom of God (Prov. 8:22–36; Ps. 88:28f.; Sir.24:3–6), the hand or arm of God (Isa.26:11; 41:15f.; 52:10; 53:1; 59:1f.; 66:1f), the Angle of the Lord (Gen. 22:11f.; 31:13; Exod. 13:21; 14:19; 23:20; Ps. 117:26; Mal .2:5f). (2) Later writings compiled "proofs" for the Trinity. The apologists centered their arguments around the plural of Genesis 1:26, "Let us make man ... " and the mysterious trio who appeared to Abraham at the oaks of Mamre (Gen. 18:1–3). In response to his typical Jew Zaccheus' interpretation of the plural address as referring to angels, the author of The Dialogue between Athanasius and Zaccheus adduced evidence from Wisdom and Word passages: in Psalm 103:24 God "made all things in wisdom," in Psalm 32:6, "The heavens were established by the Word of God," and in Proverbs 8:27–29 God and Wisdom appeared as one. He also made a convincing case from the repetition of "Lord" in Genesis 19:24–25, "And the Lord God rained brimstone and fire upon Sodom and Gomorrah by the Lord from heaven. He was careful to leave Zaccheus under no misapprehension that this implied two gods, "for the nature is the same, and there is one will and one concord." (252)–

In *The Finished Work of Christ*, Francis A. Schaeffer writes,

Because of a particular "power" (1:4). Christ's deity, to be believed, must be demonstrable. The thing that demonstrated with certainty that Christ was God was His "resurrection from (or of) the dead." (1:4). (17) (The book of John)

In *The Global God*, Aida Besancon Spencer and William David Spencer write,

The outward form was fully human. But unlike humans, Jesus never sinned (Rom. 8:3; 2 Cor. 5:21). Jesus was fully God and fully human. But, being human is not a full reflection of God. (23)

"I myself am the good shepherd," "I myself am the resurrection and the life," "I myself am the way and the truth and the life," "I myself am the true vine." When Jesus tells his fellow Jews, before Abraham was born, I myself existed" (John 8:58), his listeners knew he was claiming identity with God and they sought to stone him as a blasphemer (John 8:59). (27)

And few humans could ever have guessed that God's love would be so great that God would come in the person of Jesus to die as a final scapegoat for all transgressors. (34)

The sacrifice of God in Christ stands at the center of this mystery. (41)

God dwelled among us so that we humans might get to know God better, learn what life is all about, and become reconciled to God. Luke records that while Jesus was on earth, he demonstrated his authority, power. Identity, and concern for needy people (Luke 4:18) by the healings he did, the conversations he had, and the time he spent with people. The crowds, thereby, learned, as they grew in size, that Jesus indeed was God. (91)

The Glory of Christ author James I. Packer writes,

The Logos, he would say, is the Son. Then he would hammer home this identification in a startling way, by calling Jesus "the only God" (using a Greek adjective reserved for only sons) "who is at the Father's side," using the Greek phrase "in the Father's bosom," implying complete and unqualified intimacy; and he would round off with the thought that Jesus Christ is truly the unique revelation, demonstration, exhibition, and elucidation of God. (46)

There is one God, and there is one mediator between God and men, the man Christ Jesus. (54)

The Glory of Christ author, Jim Elliff, writes,

But in Revelation we see the most dazzling depiction of all, as the heavenly court glories in the Lamb slain, and the inhabitants of heaven sing loudly about the power and glory of the cross. (76)

And the four living creatures, each at them with six wings, are full of eyes all around and within, and day or night they never cease to say, "Holy, holy, holy, is the Lord God Almighty, who was and is and is to comer And whenever the living creatures give glory and honor and thanks to him who is seated on the throne, who lives forever and ever, the twenty-four elders fall down before him who is seated on the throne and worship him who lives forever and ever. They cast their crowns before the throne, saying, "Worthy are you, our Lord and God, to receive glory and honor and power, for you created all things, and by your will they existed and were created." (Rev. 4: 8–11) (79)

John A. Armstrong writes in *The Glory of Christ*,

"For I decided to know nothing among you except Jesus Christ and him crucified."
(I Cor 2:2) (105)

"Let all the house of Israel therefore know for certain that God has made him [Jesus] both Lord and Christ [Messiah], this Jesus whom you crucified." Acts (v. 36) (111)

The Glory of Christ author, R. Albert Mohler Jr., writes,

"And He is the image of the invisible God, the firstborn of all creation. For by Him all things were created, both in the heavens and on earth, visible and invisible, whether thrones or dominions or rulers or authorities-all things have been created through Him and for Him. He is before all things, and in Him all things hold together. He is also head of the body, the church; and He is the beginning, the firstborn from the dead, so that He Himself will come to have first place in everything." (59–60)

The New Testament makes it abundantly clear that the mediator who accomplished our salvation was fully God and fully man. (71)

As our mediator, He was fully God and fully man. He bore our griefs. He received our stripes. Indeed, He experienced temptation in every way as do we, yet without sin. (72)

James I. Packer writes in *The Glory of Christ,*

"God has highly exalted him and bestowed on him the name that is above every name [i.e., the title kurios, meaning Lord, which the Greek translation of the Old Testament used for Yahweh, God Himself], so that at the name of Jesus every knee should bow ... and every tongue confess that Jesus Christ is Lord, to the glory of God the Father" (Phil. 2:9–10). (118)

In terms of character and powers-attributes, if we wish to use the old word—the Son is eternally and unchangeably the image, or perfect match, of the Father in every respect (Col. 1:15; 2 Cor. 4:4; Heb. 1:3). In terms of personhood, the Father and the Son each exist "in" the other (John 10:38; 14:10–11; 17:21), so that "I and the Father are one" (John 10:30) and "Whoever has seen me has seen the Father" (14:9); this is Christ's own witness to the mystery of their consubstantiality. (121)

In terms, finally, of the divine program for this world and the next, it is the Father's pleasure to exalt the Son as the focus of all cosmic life and creaturely worship forever.

All things were created, and the church was redeemed
and brought into active being as His body, not only by
Him but "for him" (v, 16) that is, so that in all things He
might be "preeminent" (v. 18) "Christ Supreme." (121)

In *The Missionary Nature of the Church*, Johannes Blauw writes,

I have also been asked why I have taken the Old Testament
as my starting point. Some were of the opinion that this
wronged Jesus Christ as God's main revelation. I hasten
to declare that I, too, consider the Scriptures precious
because they testify of Jesus Christ (John 5: 39), and are
realized in Him. The Scriptures have an open horizon
turned towards Jesus Christ, but that also means that
Jesus Christ has a previous history worth investigating. It
is He who gives the Old Testament its perspective and He
cannot be understood except in the light of God's actions
in history, the history of salvation. That is why this book
has been arranged in such a way as to deal with God's
actions in history since the creation of the world. (12–13)

But it is quite plain that He who has made the nations
(Ps. 86: 9) and who has made them as His nations (Ps.
87) is also the only one who can call them to Himself.
That which will bring the world of nations to Him is
not Israel's calling them, nor her going out to them, but
exclusively the visible manifestation of the deeds of God
in and with Israel; only so will they recognize Yahweh
as their God, i.e., confess that Israel's God is their God,
the God of the whole earth, the only, God. (37)

The Messiah figure is a divine figure who will bring
to expression the actual royal lordship of God in the
future. Therefore, the Messiah is not so much the bringer
and author of salvation as He is its representative. The
Messiah is the visible manifestation of God Himself. In

the light of this statement, all the Psalms which celebrate the future royal lordship of God belong to the category of Messianic Psalms; while, moreover, Israel's kings are often provided with Messianic features, as for example Ps. 72 el al. In other words, the universal lordship of God and the lordship of the Messiah are correlates: the latter is an expression of the former, *we are* justified in concluding that the universal lordship of God, the eschatological expectation of salvation and the expectation of the Messiah belong together; they are, as it were, concentric circles, the Messiah is the center of the Israelite as well as of the universal expectation of salvation. (47)

The Messiah represents the Kingdom, the Royal Dominion of God; the Messiah is, as it were, the visible appearance of God Himself … The Messiah Himself is more a visible appearance of God than a human figure who enters the world of nations preaching. (51)

In *The Names of God*, George W. Knight writes,

When Thomas finally saw the resurrected Lord, he not only believed, but he also acknowledged Jesus as God in the Flesh. This is one of the clearest statements in all the New Testament of the divinity of Jesus and His oneness with the Father. (116)

Thomas, like all the other disciples of Jesus, had lived and worked with Him for about three years. They had walked with Him among the people, observing His miracles and listening to His teachings on the kingdom of God. But they were slow to understand that Jesus was actually God come to earth in human form. Theologians call this the doctrine of incarnation, a word that derives from a Latin term, in carne, meaning "in flesh." (116)

As the God-man, Jesus is both the all-powerful Father, for whom nothing is impossible, and the man of sorrows, who can sympathize with us in our human weakness. He is the all-sufficient Savior. (116)

Other names of God the Son that express His divinity and oneness with the Father are God Blessed For Ever (Romans 9:5), God Manifest in the Flesh (1 Timothy 3:16), God Our Saviour and True God (1 JOHN 5:20). (116)

The New Testament Documents: Are They Reliable? author, F. F. Bruce, writes.

Have the fathers and the creeds of the church outstripped the NT evidence in speaking so plainly and so often of Christ as "God"? (10)

The provocative thesis of A. C. McGiffert, that Jesus was "The God of the Early Christians, seems to have been forgotten. (11)

God in his divine essence and attributes, God who cannot be directly known. (39)

In the life of Jesus all the truth of God which had ever been communicated to men was summed up and mad perfect; in Him the eternal Word or self-expression of God had come home to the world in a real human life. (60)

Historical research is by no means excluded, for the whole point of the gospel is that in Christ the power and grace of God entered into human history to bring about the world's redemption. (67)

In *The Next Reformation: Why Evangelicals Must Embrace Postmodernity,* Carl Raschke writes,

According to Gordon R. Lewis, evangelicals have' "at least three absolutes'" a totally transcendent God; the "once-for-all, supernatural incarnation of Jesus Christ "; and "the once-for-all supernatural inscripturation of sound information in the biblical canon ..." (140)

Gonzalez writes: "Christian truth is such that it is not lost or distorted upon uniting itself with the concrete, the limited, and the transitory. On the contrary, the truth—or at least that truth which is given to men—is given precisely there when the eternal unites with the historical; where God became flesh; where a specific man, in a specific situation, is able to say: 'I am the truth.'" (209)

In *The Trinity*, Roger E. Olson and Christopher A. Hall wrote,

According to the church father Augustine anyone who denies the Trinity is in danger of losing her salvation, but anyone who tries to understand the Trinity is in danger of losing her mind. (1)

The Christian gospel is that God came among people in Jesus Christ - "Immanuel" "God with us:" It also includes the unity of God: "Hear 0 Israel, the Lord our God is one Lord:" (3)

Apart from the biblical testimony rooted in the history of salvation itself, the church as it developed would have had little motivation, need, or desire to develop a trinitarian model of God. (5)

Although there is no written word "Trinity" In the Bible, there is evidence that the concept is biblically supported in the Old Testament. (5)

It is in Jesus, "God with us;" that the Son is revealed and the Father through him. Indeed, all things have been "handed over" by the Father to the Son. "No one knows the Son except the Father, and no one knows the Father except the Son and anyone to whom the Son chooses to reveal him" (Matt. 11:27). As Gerald O'Collins comments, "This is to affirm a unique mutual knowledge and relationship of Jesus precisely as the Son to the Father, a mutual relationship out of which Jesus reveals, not a previously unknown God, but the God whom he alone knows fully and really." (7)

New Testament writers such as the apostle John insist that the incarnate Christ is actually the logos of God, present with God at the beginning and now entering the world joined to human nature (John 1:1, 14). How could the logos become a human being? John wisely does not attempt to explain how such could be the case. Apart from the events of the gospel narrative itself, John would never have pictured God in such a complex manner. Yet, precisely because of those events and their accompanying teaching, John insists on the incarnation of the pre-existent Son. Finally, John writes that it is through the preexistent logos that creation itself has taken place (John 1:3). (7)

Paul and the writer of Hebrews will also argue for the Son's pre-existence, but without using John's logos terminology. Paul writes of the Son as "the image of the invisible God, the first-born over all creation. For by him all things were created ..." (Col. 1:15–16). (7)

We have the same kind of sprinkling effect in the letters of Ignatius, bishop of Antioch. Ignatius penned these letters as he was led under Roman guard to execution in Rome. In them Ignatius employs elevated language as he speaks of the Father, Son, and Holy Spirit. For instance, in his introduction to his letter to the church in Ephesus, Ignatius writes of the Ephesians as "united and elect through genuine suffering by the will of the Father and of Jesus Christ our God" (intro.). Later in the same letter Ignatius describes Christ "as the mind of the Father" (Ephesians 1:30) (17)

Athanasius will later argue, for example, that if Christians have worshiped and continue to worship Christ, he must be considered God. To admit otherwise would be to accuse the church of continuous blasphemy in its prayer and practice, from the first century onwards. (19)

(Justin Martyr) "Therefore these words testify explicitly that He is witnessed to by Him who established these things, as deserving to be worshipped, as God and as Christ" (chapter 63). (21)

How can one best describe the relationship between the Father and the Son? Justin refers to Christ in a variety of ways, including "Lord," "God" "God the Son of God;" and "the Word." (21)

Irenaeus, like almost all church fathers, was deeply concerned to protect the transcendence of the Father, while equally insisting that God has entered his world in the incarnation of the Son. (28)

Irenaeus writes that "Jesus Christ was not a mere man ... but was very God." Irenaeus' christology from Against Heresies can be supplemented by Fragments from the Lost Writings of Irenaeus, 52–54, AN, vol. 1, pp. 576–77. (290)

These fragments are largely christological in nature, clearly representing Irenaeus' consistent contention that the Father and Son are one God, not two, and surely not part of a chain of aeons or angels - a common gnostic contention. (29)

The Universe Next Door: A Basic Worldview Catalog author, James W. Sire, writes,

> Human beings can know both the world around them and God himself because God has built into them the capacity to do so and because he takes an active role in communicating with them. (30)

> But in these last days he has spoken to us by a Son, whom he appointed the heir of all things. … "He reflects the glory of God and bears the very stamp of his nature" (Heb. 1:2–3). Jesus Christ is God's ultimate special revelation. Because Jesus Christ was very God of very God he showed us what God is like more fully than can any other form of revelation. Because Jesus was also completely man, he spoke more clearly to us than can any other form of revelation. (32)

> The fullest embodiment of the good, however, is Jesus Christ. His is the complete man, humanity as God would have it be. (36)

> But for a theist God has also revealed himself in words— oppositional, verbalized revelation to his prophets and the various biblical writers. And, theists maintain, God has also revealed himself in his Son, Jesus—the "Word became flesh (Jan 1:14)." (46)

In *Total Truth Liberating Christianity from Its Cultural Captivity*, Nancy R. Pearcey writes,

> Jesus took on a human body yet had no sin. The sheer, monumental fact that God Himself took on human form speaks decisively of the dignity of the body. For

Greek thinkers, the most shocking claim Christians made was that God had become a historical person, who could be seen, heard, and touched. Rational inquiry could no longer simply reject the world of the senses but had to take account of history—events in time and space like Christ's incarnation, death, and resurrection. (76)

Picture the world as God's territory right of Creation. Because of the Fall, it has been invaded and occupied by Satan and his minions, who constantly wage war against God's people. At the central turning point in history, God Himself, the second person of the trinity, enters the world in the Person of Jesus Christ and deals Satan a deathblow through His Resurrection. (90–91)

For example, in the twelfth century Anselm had offered a case for salvation that was concise and logic: *Because* human beings sinned, therefore a human being had to render payment. *However,* the debt we owe God is so great that only God Himself is able to pay it. *Therefore,* God became a human being in order to pay the price exacted by divine justice. Anselm's point was that God's plan of salvation makes perfect sense. (100)

In *True Spirituality*, Francis A. Schaffer writes,

Now the death of the Lord Jesus is absolutely unique. It is substitutionary. There is no death like Jesus' death. There is no parallel death to Jesus' death-this must stand as absolute in our thinking. His substitutionary death on the cross, in space and time in history, had infinite value because of who he is as God. Thus nothing need be added to the substitutionary value of his death, nor can anything be added. He died once for all. (22)

What we see him to be after his resurrection, Paul insists, *we shall be*. When I consider the resurrection of

Jesus Christ, not merely in the world of religious ideas or ideals, but in the world of space and time and reality, I have the promise from the hand of God himself that I will be so raised from death. (34)

In *Truth Decay*, Douglas Groothuis writes,

Consider Jesus' identity as God incarnate. One can formulate this truth in various propositions, each with a greater level of conceptual sophistication." Jesus is truly divine and truly human. Jesus is one person with two natures: divine and human. Jesus' two natures express a hypostatic union of divinity and humanity in one person. (118)

All three statements are objectively true because they correspond with the reality of Jesus Christ as God incarnate. These propositions "themselves express final truth, "but they each do so with a different level of conceptual content and specification. None of these statements supplies the comprehensive truth of the incarnation (nor does the Council of Chalcedon's highly nuanced articulation), but they are all equally true and biblically congruent. These truths may serve as a foundation for further knowledge and clarification, but they succeed in their intent to be universally true. "Universal intent" trying to get reality right-Grenz to the contrary, is not sufficient for theologizing, although it is necessary. (118)

Moreover, as Henry and others have developed at length, John's Gospel (1:1–3) refers to the preincarnate Christ as the Logos (or Word). This means, among other things, that the personal Word is intelligible and rational, that he created a knowable world peopled by creatures who can know truth through rationality. The Word is

God communicating, God speaking. Early Christian apologists employed this notion to argue that any truth discovered by non-Christian philosophers was only possible because of God, the Logos. (122)

McGrath seems sanguine about the prospects of postmodernity, but he fails to note that Christian theology is a metanarrative based on God's self-disclosure. The postmodernists on which McGrath relies see the collapse of Enlightenment rationalism as the end of all metanarratives. If Christians cannot appeal to universal standards of rationality and morality in their apologetic and their theological articulations, the postmodernist criticism of metanarratives ends up eroding the Christianity that believers seek to present to the postmodern world. The very concept of divine revelation presupposes that those who receive that revelation do have some access to objective reality. God has made himself known in creation, conscience, Christ and the Scriptures. Followers of Christ have the privilege of knowing that Jesus is Lord; others do not (1 Cor. 8:6). Jesus' lordship covers all of reality, and all wisdom and knowledge is found in Christ (Col. 1:15–17; 2:3). We know only in part in this life (1 Cor. 13:12), but we can know truly because we have been privileged with knowledge from God, the omniscient and omnipotent Revealer. (130)

In our pluralistic and postmodern context, it is helpful to articulate Christian truth claims in relation to opposing views-not to be contentious but to clarify what is being put forth and what is not. Any truth claim negates every proposition that denies it. This is the logic of antithesis, as discussed in chapter three. For instance, if Jesus is God incarnate, then he is not (1) a mere prophet of Allah (Islam), (2) a misguided reformer (Judaism), (3) an avatar of Brahman (Hinduism), (4) a manifestation of God (Baha'i Faith), (5) a God-realized guru (New Age), (6) an inspired but not divine social prophet (theological liberalism), and so on. (166)

Given his incomparable claims and credentials, Jesus' identity is best explained by the historic Christian claim that he was God incarnate. Other explanations—that he was a guru, a social reformer or an impostor—do not fit the facts. As God incarnate, Jesus is the only avenue of spiritual liberation and escape from divine judgment and, therefore, should be followed as Lord of the universe and of one's life. (181)

Apologists should not only defend the rationality of Jesus as Lord but, also encourage unbelievers to expose themselves to the Gospel narratives (about which many are ignorant). Here we find many unforgettable micronarratives inseparably wedded to the metanarrative of God's grand design for the universe, the Word become flesh for the purpose of personal and cosmic redemption (Jn.1:14). There is an apologetic force simply in the thoughtful reading of the accounts of Jesus' incomparable life, as I experienced myself in 1976, Questions regarding specific apologetic issues may be generated out of such exposure to the reliability of the Gospel accounts (see point 6), but direct exposure to the life of Christ through Scripture is in itself a powerful apologetic that must not be ignored by the apt apologist. (181–182)

I assume you would ask if so much information is necessary to show that Jesus is God. The answer is yes because I am not interested in giving you my personal opinion; I want to give only the best information, supporting these positions by those closest to Jesus, the apostles, and some of the greatest Christian writers.

Now we know we cannot communicate directly with God the Father. We know Jesus has always existed. We know Jesus is the communicator of God the Father, in the Old Testament and in the New Testament. We know Jesus created the heavens and the earth and everything else, including you and me and every other human being. We know the mystery hidden for thousands of years is the birth of Jesus here on earth. We know that the birth of Jesus was not a natural human birth but a spiritual process. We know that Jesus being the Son of God the Father is not to be compared to a son who is born to a natural mother and father. Jesus is not a son of God the Father; he is *the only Son* of God the Father. And now we know that Jesus is God!

Part 4

He must be Preeminent in All Things

Jesus must be preeminent in everything that we do or say, not just on Sunday or when you think about spiritual things. It definitely should not just be when you think you or someone else is about to die—like the person who thought he was about to crash in his airplane and said, "Right then and there, I prayed to God," which, by the way, was his *imaginary friend*. Here is information about Jesus's preeminence:

Ante-Nicene Fathers, volume 1, contains Ireneus's "Against Heresies." In book III, he writes,

> But let us revert to the same line of argument [hitherto pursued]. For when it has been manifestly declared, that they who were the preachers of the truth and the apostles of liberty termed no one else God, or named him Lord, except the only true God the Father, and His Word, who has the preeminence in all things; it shall then be clearly proved, that they (the apostles) confessed as the Lord God Him who was the Creator of heaven and earth, who also spoke with Moses, gave to him the dispensation of

the law, and who called the fathers; and that they knew no other. The opinion of the apostles, therefore, and of those (Mark and Luke) who learned from their words, concerning God, has been made manifest. (440)

Ante-Nicene Fathers, volume 5, contains "The Treatises of Cyprian," in which he writes,

> Also Paul to the Colossians: "Who is the image of the invisible God, and the first-born of every creature." Also, in the same place: "The first-born from the dead, that He might in all things become the holder of the pre-eminence." (516)

In *Baker's Dictionary of Theology*, Everett F. Harrison writes,

> Pauls' head-on clash with incipient Gnosticism (q.v.) evokes his classic statement concerning the pre-eminence of Christ in Col. 1:13 ff. Gnostic stress on the exaltation of angels and the need for a sub-divine mediator in creation to bridge the gap between the perfect God and imperfect matter made It necessary for Paul to highlight the differences between Gnosticism and Christianity with a concise statement of the lordship of Christ. The climax of the passage is the final clause of Col. I: 18. "that in all things he might have pre-eminence, "be first, have first place. (417)

> The evidences of Christ's per-eminence are manifold: he alone is the image of the invisible God. he is the pre-existent creator and the perpetual sustainer of the universe, the great Head of creation. he is the triumphant Head of the church, the first conqueror of death. he is the possessor of all fullness—whether of virtue or blessing, especially the blessing of reconciliation to God. (417)

In *The New Testament Introduction*, Donald Guthrie, BD, MTh, PhD, writes,

> Paul has two main problems to settle, one doctrinal, concerning the Person of Christ, the other practical, respecting the life of the Christian. (551)

> The Epistle contains a high Christology. Christ is preeminent over all other creatures and over creation itself. In fact, all things were not only created by Him but for Him. He is seen at the center of the universe sovereign over all principalities and powers, over all agencies, that is to say, which might challenge His authority. Not only so, He is the Image of God and the Possessor of the fulness (pleroma) of God and these statements could not fail to exalt Him to equality with God. (551)

> Clearly Paul's purpose is to demonstrate the immeasurable superiority of Christ, as contrasted with the inadequate presentation of Him being advocated by the Colossian false teachers. (551)

There is no need for anyone to misunderstand. God is not a complete mystery. He is not some kind of imaginary friend, floating around in the clouds. He is not someone you can only know when you have chills up and down your spine or only when you are dying. We can know God the Father, thankfully, by a true and honest understanding of or Lord and our God Jesus. Only through him can God the Father be known.

Part 5

A Brief Understanding of the Solution.

Now that we have the facts, it's time to discuss the solution that will give you a foundation for life and also will give you the peace and contentment that every person needs to endure the hardships and to enjoy the pleasures of life.

When I was in college, one of my professors told us, "Never present a serious problem without also presenting a serious solution." The solution is to have a solid foundation for your life, which will give you the peace that surpasses all understanding. The solution is to follow the Lord Jesus—in other words, be a Christian.

Christianity is the solution, and I would like to use two illustrations. I don't know where these illustrations originated, but I always have remembered them. I hope you will too.

A Christian and an atheist were talking, and the atheist said, "What if you live your life according to all the rules and regulations of Christianity, avoiding all the things in life that most people think are fun and enjoyable, and at the end of your life, you find out that there is no Lord or God and no afterlife?"

"Well," the Christian said, "if all you say is true, I would still be able to say that because I was a Christian and my parents were Christians. I

learned at an early age to do the best that I could in school and to treat others with respect and dignity. I learned not to lie, cheat, or steal, and I learned all the other good things that Christianity teaches. Because of those teachings, I believe that I have become a better student, a better person, a better employee, a better husband, a better father, and a better citizen. I've lived, to the best of my ability, a peaceful and content life, just thinking that the promises the Lord gave to me would be kept, such as eternal life."

The atheist said nothing after that.

A young person was graduating from high school, and a friend asked. "What will you do now?"

The young person said, "I guess I will go to college and obtain a degree."

"And then what?" the friend asked.

"I guess I will have to decide on which occupation to pursue and will probably have another few years of education to contend with," the young person said.

"And then what?"

"Then I guess I will get married and get ahead in my occupation."

"And then what?" the friend asked.

"I guess my spouse and I will have children and live our lives."

"And then what?" the friend asked.

"I guess I will just get older," the young person said.

"And then what?"

With a bit of anger, the young person said, "I guess I will die."

In a very serious voice, the friend asked, "And then what?"

The young person had no answer.

Please understand that *no one can make judgments* about Christianity based on the actions of any one Christian. Christians are flawed human beings, like everyone else. Most Christians are trying to follow what the Lord Jesus has instructed them to do. They are no different from any other person, with regard to human weaknesses.

I will tell you a true story that happened to me. One afternoon I was having lunch with two prominent ministers. I was new to the ministry—this was my first placement—and I felt a bit out of place during this lunch. These two men had been Christians from childhood, and I had only been a Christian for about three years. (Before that, I had grown up in a home that was, let's say, the opposite of Christianity.)

During the conversation at lunch, one of them said they both had to be examples to the others in their congregations, and I think they really believed it. That statement went through my heart like a knife. I could not believe that these two men honestly thought they could be the example to others, no less an example to an entire church.

I mustered the courage to confront them by saying, "I do not mean to be rude, but I disagree that you have to be the examples to your churches."

"Why?" they asked.

I said, "I know of only one example that we, as flawed humans, must look to, and that is our Lord. If you or anyone else thinks they are examples for others to follow, they are seriously mistaken. Why? Because we are all just people who make serious mistakes every day. You cannot be an example to others because you are the same as they are. On the other hand, if others tell you that you have been an example to them, that's a good thing. We can all hope to be examples to others, but we can never imply that we *are* the example for others. That said, remember when you make judgments about Christianity, use the only true and perfect example—Jesus. Do not think that Christians are hypocrites because we are all hypocrites in one way or another."

Some people say they are not Christians, but we can see that they live by Christian values. Values do not just materialize in someone's brain; they were given to us by the Lord. Either you follow values that exist, or you do not. Christians have an objective set of values by which they *try* to live, but others do not have an objective set of values that they live by. They just make up their values as they go along, living their lives without any basis to refer to. That is a major problem we face in our world today, if not the greatest problem.

Remember that most people who say they believe in God are what I call Goddians—they believe in God but cannot explain why. Christians, on the other hand, know exactly what they mean when they say the word *God* because they follow a real historical person named Jesus the Christ, who has explained to them who God is. Christians try to be as the word *Christian* implies, and that is Christlike. The Goddians try to be Godlike, but they cannot comprehend God without understanding who Jesus is. I personally feel a great deal of sorrow for all of them. Christians know what Jesus taught, and we know that he is real and alive today, which makes our faith objective, not subjective.

What do you believe most people would do today when confronted with a moral dilemma? Let us use lying as an example. I read a book once that did its best to convince readers that lying was necessary at certain times. The writer used an example of a terrible situation, where a mother was out in the wilderness and was confronted with cold-blooded killers. She saw them coming, so she hid her two young children. Somehow, the killers knew that she had children, and they wanted to take them. The killers demanded that she tell them where the children were.

To protect her children, she told the killers that earlier that morning, their father had taken them in to town. That was a lie! Question: was she right to lie in that situation? You were probably anticipating my answer to be no, but my answer is yes. Under that kind of duress, anyone would do what was needed to protect their children.

Although the situation seamed to demand a lie, that does not mean that lying is justified in the eyes of our Lord. The mother, at the time she lied, more than likely felt a twinge in her soul and probably felt bad about lying. That, my friends, is what is called repentance, and therefore, she could have a clear conscience. If someone lies and does not care and has no remorse for lying, that person is a troubled person. Lying, like many other absolutes, is wrong but forgivable.

Many people without any moral base to rely on seem to think that they can lie if it benefits them personally. I believe that every person, especially politicians, should incorporate the following saying into their lives—better yet, have it branded into their brain. The saying is as follows: A half-truth is a total lie.

If a person does not tell the truth, the whole truth, and nothing but the truth, it is a lie.

We always need to tell the complete truth. The answer to the moral dilemma mentioned above is that most people would lie because they do not have a sound basis to rely on for difficult answers. Christianity can provide you with an absolute basis for your life, which will allow you to live a peaceful and content life. The solution is Jesus!

We know that we can't communicate with God the Father directly. We know Jesus has always existed. We know Jesus is the communicator of God the Father, in the Old Testament and in the New Testament. We know Jesus created the heavens and the earth and everything else, including you and me and every other human being. We know the mystery hidden for thousands of years is the birth of Jesus here on earth. We know that the birth of Jesus was not a natural human birth but a spiritual process. We know that Jesus's being the Son of God the Father is not to be compared to a son born to a natural mother and father. Jesus is not a son of God the Father. He is the *only Son* of God the Father. And now we know that Jesus is God.

We also know we should not judge Christianity by the actions of any one person because people are not our examples. We all are imperfect human beings. We know that Goddians follow their imaginary god, and Christians follow Jesus the Christ. We know most people make difficult moral decisions based on the situation in which they find themselves.

Remember that a half truth is a total lie. Remember too that many people have become *radical irrational individuals*, who make most of their decisions on religion without bothering to investigate the facts pertaining to that religion.

As a solution for each one of us to live a peaceful and content life, during the good times and the bad times, we all need a solid foundation that does not ever move and is stable under all circumstances. That foundation is Christianity—Jesus the Christ.

When I said that Christianity is often seen as a garbage dump, that's because that's the perception that people have of Christianity. Christianity has been taken hostage by every kind of evil device. Christianity has been used and extremely manipulated in every way possible to include mass suicide and murder by many so-called Christians. The most notable event where a man used Christianity as an evil tool was the event at Jonestown in Guyana, where people were controlled by religious leader Jim Jones. Approximately 909 people died by drinking tainted Kool-Aid, and some were also murdered.

There are plenty of other incidents like the Jones incident. Lying for money seems to be the most attractive way for most of the so-called Christian ministers, preachers, evangelists, and pastors to participate in. As I have mentioned, if you want a deeper understanding of this topic, read *Blessed* by Kate Bowler.

Then we have what I call the *erroneous zone* so-called Christian ministers, preachers, evangelists, and pastors, who love the money but also will make you happy and make you feel good about yourself, and then ask for money. Then we have the God-told-me so-called Christian ministers, preachers, evangelists, and pastors, who want others to believe that they personally have talked to God. If God is talking to all these people, can you tell me why we need Jesus, or the apostles, or the Bible. Would it not be better to get up-to-date information directly from God?

Why is this kind of evil taking over Christianity? It's because radical irrational individualism has taken over every aspect of American life. Anyone today can open what is called a Christian church. Do an internet search using the word *church*, and see what comes up. I believe you will find every kind of church you can imagine, including the church of Satanism. Educational intellectualism and reality has been replaced with thinking that anything is acceptable, and especially in the realm of religion.

People should take the time and make an effort to educate themselves and to confer with knowledgeable and well-educated individuals who have proven themselves by their actions and their knowledge. It's important to know that these individuals do not have any ulterior motives, such as money, their own personal pride, or any other personal gain. You should know that the only thing they want to do is to help you understand that Christianity is the foundation that will provide you with the peace and contentment that we all are looking for and need so very much in our lives today.

Part 6

A Brief Understanding of Real Christianity

Let's look back to the beginning of Christianity. What did Christianity look like some two thousand years ago? The Lord returned to his original place. He was not dead, and he had left men and women here on earth with his teachings. He guided them personally to teach the world his good news. Within a short time, this good-news message had touched the entire world. People came together to learn and participate in helping others to understand the new life-changing message. By the thousands and then by the hundreds of thousands, people happily comprehended the message of the Lord and became true followers of Jesus, our Lord and our God.

These people learned to love each other as the Lord had taught. They wanted to be with each other to continue to learn the Lord's will and, when needed, to help each other as best as they could. This was an assembly of individuals who did not want to be radical irrational individuals anymore; they wanted to be a part of each other's lives and glorify Jesus together. That sounds like a church, and it was.

Remember that there will never be a perfect church of any kind because Jesus taught that there would always be those who are not dedicated to the Lord within the assembly or the church.

Many years passed, and Paul and other true followers of the Lord put the writings of the apostles together, with the guidance of our Lord. These were the scriptures, better known as the New Testament in the Bible. Here we have instructions to all the people of the world, in written contractual form, directly from the Lord. Fortunately for all of us, these writing have never been distorted or destroyed in over two thousand years. There were many problems along the way. The church was fractured and has continued to fracture, up to our present time. Why? Because people wanted to do it their way instead of the Lord's way.

Part 7

How to Obtain a Personal Relationship with Our Lord and our God Jesus

A person who wants a personal relationship with the Lord must take an active part—intellectually, emotionally, and physically. He or she must obtain that relationship in the same way that every other person we read about in the scriptures has done.

There are seven incidences in the scriptures of individuals establishing a personal relationship with our Lord, and they all followed the same pattern. That pattern includes four personal actions.

The first action is that they believed. Belief can be a simple thing, or it can be a very deep, personal thing. A simple belief can be something like saying, "I believe in fairy tales," or "I believe in the creature Big Foot," or "I believe in the Easter Bunny."

I will try to explain deep belief by using an old song by Don Williams, "I Believe in Love." He sings, "I believe in babies. I believe in Mom and Dad. I believe in old folks, and I believe in love." Those things are deep beliefs, which a person must have for our Lord before he or she can have a personal relationship with him. The belief must be based on real, intellectual information and a deep, sincere belief.

The second action all the individuals engaged in was nonconformance. The scriptures teach us not to conform to this world but to be transformed by the renewing of our minds. This is a very difficult, if not impossible, thing to accomplish in the present time, considering the tainted environment we live in. Whatever we do or wherever we go, we are saturated with things that are inconsistent with what the Lord teaches. One example that I recognized while driving along a main road was the number of advertisement signs. Some lit up electrically with great color and brightness, and most of them advertised things that are not very good for us, physically or mentally. We are continually bombarded from all sources to conform to the ways of the world. The difficulty of nonconformance is a reality, but the Lord expects us to do our absolute best to do what he wants, not what the world or our country wants. All the individuals who wanted a personal relationship with Jesus needed to have a lifestyle change and nonconformity.

The third action all the individuals engaged in was a complete openness about the Lord. The people of the first three centuries were so very proud to be called Christians—so proud that during three times of great persecution by the Roman government, they were willing to die rather than deny that they were followers of Jesus. The Roman government gave most of them the opportunity to live if they would worship both the Roman gods and Jesus, but they refused, and they suffered brutal punishment and death. We are so very fortunate, at least right now, that we have the privilege of worshiping our Lord whenever and wherever we would like. A person who wants to establish a personal relationship with Jesus must be proud of him and not be apprehensive to let others know.

The fourth action a person must take to establish a personal relationship with our Lord and our God is to be baptized. This action is often the most difficult for people to understand because of the garbage dump of religious opinions we have been exposed to all our lives. Let's look at the meaning of the word *baptized*. Baptized is a Greek word that was made to sound as much like English as possible. I would encourage you to look in a dictionary of theology to get the true meaning of the word. I will give you the meaning of the word from Baker's *Dictionary of Theology*: "Baptism deriving from the Greek *baptisma*, "baptism" denotes the action of washing or plunging in water, which from the earliest days has been used as the rite of Christian initiation."

The meaning and proper administration of baptism was changed around AD 300. It's easy to understand why others do not understand the true meaning of the word. The scriptures have not changed the meaning of the word; people have. Why? Convenience! Why would anyone want to be dunked under water if all they needed to do was to have some water poured on their heads or just have someone sprinkle some water on them. Makes sense to me. The problem is that human sense is not what the Lord and the apostles said, taught, and demonstrated to us.

Jesus demonstrated the administration of baptism when he came to John the Baptist, who was at the River Jordan, baptizing others. Jesus went into the river, and John baptized him. Why did our Lord and our God go into the river? Because the word baptism means "to plunge something under the water." I am sure if baptism meant pouring or sprinkling water on someone's head, plenty of the people on the shore would have had some water that John could have used. Being baptized in the Jordan River was demonstrated by our Lord and our God. Baptizing infants is a total misunderstanding; baptizing infants is nowhere to be found in the scriptures. We have the examples of seven conversions in the scriptures, and all demonstrate the same administration of baptism as our Lord.

One example is well worth looking at. A person of some importance came to Jerusalem to celebrate the Jewish holiday. On his way back to his place of origin, while being driven in his coach, he was reading the scriptures. The next thing he knew, a man named Philip was there with him, and Philip heard him reading the book of Isaiah. Philip asked him if he understood what he was reading, and the man said that he did not. He invited Philip into the coach to give him the understanding he needed.

The scripture that he was reading was in the Old Testament, and it was about Jesus. Philip told him all about Jesus and the actions that a person needed to take to secure a personal relationship with our Lord and our God. Philip explained everything, including baptism, and while they were riding, this person said, "Look! Water! What prevents me from being baptized?" He ordered the coach to stop, and they both went down into the water. Philip baptized the man.

My point is that surely they had water with them, surely enough to pour or sprinkle some water on his head, so why did they both go into the water? The only reason it could have been is that *baptism* means to plunge or immerse something underwater. This has always been a good example to help others understand the true administration of baptism.

The apostle Paul describes baptism as being buried with Christ into his death (under the water) and being raised up as Christ was raised from the dead (resurrected) so we too might walk in newness of life.

The apostle Peter explains baptism by saying that Noah and his family were brought to safety through the water, and just like them, baptism now saves you. It is an appeal to God the Father for a clean conscience through the resurrection of our Lord and our God, Jesus the Christ.

To summarize, those who want a personal relationship with our Lord and our God need to (1) truly and deeply and sincerely believe Jesus; (2) not conform to this world but be transformed by the renewing of the mind; (3) be openly and truly proud of our Lord, and (4) be baptized in the same way that Jesus, the apostles, and all others were baptized from the beginning of Christianity.

What is so great about being a Christian anyway?

As a Christian, we have the Lord's forgiveness of our sins—past, present, and future. A Christian is given the gift of the Holy Spirit internally, as a helper. Christians are *given the gift of eternal life* at the same time they take the appropriate actions to establish a personal relationship with our Lord and our God. Christians have the foundation on which to live that gives them the truth, personal peace, strength, and contentment to live their lives.

What does forgiveness of sin really mean? Not like human beings, our Lord and our God forgives and forgets our sin completely and continually past, present, and future. Not understanding this is robbing Christians of one of the most wonderful promises the Lord has given them. The scripture clearly addressed this issue in the book of Romans 5–6.

As an illustration, when a child is very young and has a temper tantrum, we parents do not consider the tantrum as a sin that we cannot forgive, even when that child has another temper tantrum an hour later. We forgive and forget the first tantrum immediately, and the second, and the third, and so on. Why? Because we understand the processes of growing and maturing, and we love the child. Of course we are not children, but to our Lord and our God, according to many scriptures, the use of the word *child* seems to imply the Lord thinks about us as children. The forgiveness of sin continually and the absence of guilt in our lives is an unbelievably beautiful gift called grace.

The gift of the Holy Spirit is given to all people when they solidify their personal relationships with the Lord. When I was taught about the Holy Spirit, the first thing the professor said was that neither he nor anyone else knew everything about the Holy Spirit. We are limited in our understanding of the Holy Spirit, but we do know that we are told the Holy Spirit is our helper in all things—another gift from our Lord.

We are *given* the gift of eternal life. This must be emphasized over and over again to make sure all those who have developed a personal relationship with our Lord and our God understand. The greatest gift ever given in the history of the world has been given to them by our Lord and our God, Jesus, which is eternal life! A true gift is given without any conditions attached. A true gift is given with gladness. A true gift is given with unconditional love. No person can earn a true gift. No person can buy a true gift. No person can reciprocate in any way. No matter what you may think, no matter what you believe, no matter what you may feel, our Lord has *given* to those who have honestly accepted him, as the scriptures tells us to, the greatest gifts that have ever been given in the history of our world—the gift of forgiveness of our sins, the gift of the Holy Spirit, and the gift of eternal life. All the Lord's teachings and these unbelievable gifts are the foundation that will give you the peace and contentment that we all strive for in our lives.

The Lord has given us one more gift, and that is the gift of his return to this world at some time. When? No one knows, but we must be ready to greet him at any time. It could be right now, or tonight as we sleep, or not even in our lifetimes, but he does not break his promises. Either we will meet him after our own deaths, which can be today or a hundred years from now, or at his return. Please understand that as a true Christian, there is no fear of death or of our Lord's coming, just the receiving of the gifts he has promised.

We know we cannot communicate with God the Father directly. We know Jesus has always existed. We know Jesus is the communicator of God the Father, in the Old Testament and in the New Testament. We know Jesus created the heavens and the earth and everything else, including you and me and every other human being. We know the mystery that was hidden for thousands of years is the birth of Jesus here on earth. We know that the birth of Jesus was not a natural human birth but was a spiritual process. We know that Jesus being the Son of God the Father is not to be compared with a son's birth to a natural mother and father. Jesus is not a son of God the Father. He is the *only Son* of God the Father.

We know that Jesus is God! We know that we should not judge Christianity by the actions of any one person because people are not our examples. We know that we all are imperfect human beings. We know that Goddians follow their imaginary god, and Christians follow Jesus the Christ. We know most people make difficult moral decisions based on the situation in which they find themselves. We also know that a half truth is a total lie.

We know many people today have become radical irrational individuals, who make most of their decisions, especially in the realm of religion, without bothering to investigate the facts or the truth pertaining to that religion. We also know that the solution to life's troubles is Christianity, which will give each one of us the peace, strength, and contentment all humans are looking for.

We now know the process that the scriptures teach us to obtain a true personal relationship with our Lord and our God. We know we need to use our true intellect and our emotions, so we can honestly believe in Jesus. We know not to be conformed to the ways of this world but to be transformed to the ways of our Lord.

We know what actions we all must take, just as all others have taken, as the scriptures teach in every case. We know we must be buried with Jesus in baptism. We know that we have the wonderful and peaceful promises that our Lord and our God Jesus has given us—the forgiveness of our sins, past, present and future. We know we have the gift of the

Holy Spirit to support us in our time of need. We know we have the gift of eternal life. We also know that Jesus will be back at any time that he chooses. We know we never need to be afraid of death or of Jesus's Second Coming.

Please do not be a radical irrational individual, and do not think that you can answer every question by what you think or feel or believe. Listen to Jesus.

A Brief Supplement

Now that you have the facts from the most intellectual and prolific writers of the earliest centuries and from those who were the closest to Jesus and the apostles. Remember these facts were not my personal opinions.

I can now be a bit more personal. By the way, when I say *you* have facts, I am referring mainly to the individuals who are so very close to my wife's and my heart—our children, our grandchildren, and our great-grandchildren, although I hope that this information will benefit as many people as possible.

I love my family and friends with more than just a deep emotional affection. I always include my wife. I love them with a love that requires me to give them the information that will give them a life with the most contentment, peace, and happiness, although it is extremely difficult at times and sometimes confrontational. The truth needs to be presented to them, regardless of their personal opinions or feelings.

I have presented the facts and the truth that I have learned over the last fifty years. Our Lord and our God has left all of us the truth. If we all thoroughly study the information the Lord has left us, I am sure that we all will have a solid foundation and absolutes to guide and protect us.

I see myself much more like a soldier than a patient, loving counselor. If I was driving to a destination and got a flat tire, I would not stand by the car and contemplate why I got the flat. I would just fix it and get going.

I'm reminded of the old TV show *Dragnet*. When the detectives were investigating a crime, and the person they were questioning would talk about something that did not pertain to their investigation, the detectives would say, "We want the facts, nothing but the facts." That is what I have tried to do in this book. My opinion, your opinion, other opinions are of no value to anyone unless they contain the "facts, nothing but the facts" that our Lord and our God has given us. *Do all things through Jesus our Lord and our God.*

BIBLIOGRAPHY

Africanus. Julius. "The Extant Writings of Julius Africanus." In *Ante-Nicene Fathers*, vol. 6. Peabody: Hendrickson Publishers Inc., 2004.

Alexander of Alexander. "Epistle on the Arian Heresy and the Deposition of Arius." In *Ante-Nicene Fathers*, vol. 6. Peabody: Hendrickson Publishers Inc., 2004.

Alexandrinus, Clemens. "Fragments of." In *Ante-Nicene Fathers*, vol. 2. Peabody: Hendrickson Publishers, Inc., 2004.

Alexandrinus, Clemens. "Who Is the Rich Man That Will Be Saved?" In *Ante-Nicene Fathers*, vol. 2. Peabody: Hendrickson Publishers, Inc., 2004.

Archelaus. "The Acts of the Disputation with the Heresiarch Manes." In *Ante-Nicene Fathers*, vol. 6. Peabody: Hendrickson Publishers Inc., 2004.

Aristides. "The Apology of Aristides the Philosopher." In *Ante-Nicene Fathers*, vol. 9. Peabody: Hendrickson Publishers, Inc., 2004.

Armstrong, John H., ed. *The Glory of Christ*. Wheaton: Crossway Books, 2002.

Arnobius. "The Seven Books of Arnobius against the Heathen." In *Ante-Nicene Fathers*, vol. 6. Peabody: Hendrickson Publishers Inc., 2004.

Athenagoras the Athenian. *Ante-Nicene Fathers,* vol. 2, Peabody, Massachusetts: Hendrickson Publishers, Inc., 2004.

Athenagoras. "A Plea for the Christians by Athenagoras the Athenian." In *Ante-Nicene Fathers*, vol. 2. Peabody: Hendrickson Publishers, Inc., 2004.

Baxter, Batsell Barrett. *I Believe Because*. Grand Rapids: Baker Book House, Co., 1971.

Blauw, Johannes. *The Missionary Nature of the Church*. Cambridge: The Lutterworth Press, 1962.

Bowler, Kate. *Blessed*. New York: Oxford University Press, 2003.

Bruce. F. F. *Jesus & Christian Origins Outside the New Testament*. Grand Rapids: William B. Eerdmans Publishing Co., 1974.

Bruce, F. F. *The New Testament Documents: Are They Reliable?* Michigan: William B. Eerdmans Publishing, Inc., 1974.

Caius. "Fragments of Caius." In *Ante-Nicene Fathers*, vol. 5. Peabody: Hendrickson Publishers Inc., 2004.

Clemens Alexandrinus. "On the First Epistle of Peter." In *Ante-Nicene Fathers*, vol. 2. Peabody: Hendrickson Publishers, Inc., 2004.

Clement. "The First Epistle of Clement to the Corinthians." In *Ante-Nicene Fathers*, vol. 1. Grand Rapids: Wm. B. Eerdmans Publishing Co., 1996.

Clement. "The Recognitions of Clement." In *Ante-Nicene Fathers*, vol. 8. Peabody: Hendrickson Publishers, Inc., 2004.

Clement of Alexandria. "Exhortation to the Heathen." In *Ante-Nicene Fathers*, vol. 2. Peabody: Hendrickson Publishers, Inc., 2004.

Clement of Alexandria. "The Instructor." In *Ante-Nicene Fathers*, vol. 2. Peabody: Hendrickson Publishers, Inc., 2004.

Clement of Alexandria. "The Stromata, or Miscellanies." In *Ante-Nicene Fathers*, vol. 2. Peabody: Hendrickson Publishers, Inc., 2004.

Commodianus. "The Instructions of Commodianus." In *Ante-Nicene Fathers*, vol. 4. Peabody: Hendrickson Publishers Inc., 2004.

Craig. William Lane. *Reasonable Faith*. Wheaton: Crossway Books, 2008.

Cyprian. "The Epistles of Cyprian." In *Ante-Nicene Fathers*, vol. 5. Peabody: Hendrickson Publishers Inc., 2004.

Cyprian. "The Treatises of Cyprian." In *Ante-Nicene Fathers*, vol. 5. Peabody: Hendrickson Publishers, Inc., 2004.

Dionysius of Rome. "Against the Sabellians." In *Ante-Nicene Fathers*, vol. 7. Peabody: Hendrickson Publishers Inc., 2004.

"Encyclical Epistle of the Church at Smyrna Concerning the Martyrdom of the Holy Polycarp." In *Ante-Nicene Fathers*, vol. 1. Grand Rapids: Wm. B. Eerdmans Publishing Co., 1996.

"Epistles of Clement." In *Ante-Nicene Fathers*, vol. 9. Peabody: Hendrickson Publishers Inc., 2004.

Erickson, Millard J. *God in Three Persons*. Grand Rapids: Baker Books, 1995.

Felix, Minucius. "The Octavius of Minucius Felix." In *Ante-Nicene Fathers*, vol. 4. Peabody: Hendrickson Publishers Inc., 2004.

Floyd, Harvey. *Is the Holy Spirit for Me?* Nashville: 20th Century Christian, 1987.

Geisler, Norman L. *Philosophy of Religion*. Michigan: Zondervan Publish House, 1974.

Green, Michael. *Evangelism in the Early Church*. Grand Rapids: William B. Eerdmans Publishing Co., 2004.

Groothuis, Douglas. *Truth Decay*. Downers Grove: InterVarsity Press, 2000.

Guthrie, Donald. *New Testament Introduction*. Downers Grove: InterVarsity Press, 1973.

Harris, Murray J. *Jesus as God*. Grand Rapids: Baker Books, 1992.

Harrison, Everett F. *Baker's Dictionary of Theology*. Michigan: Baker Book House, 1973.

Hinson, E. Glenn. *The Evangelization of the Roman Empire*. Macon: Mercer University Press, 1987.

Hippolytus. "Appendix to the Works of Hippolytus." In *Ante-Nicene Fathers*, vol. 5. Peabody: Hendrickson Publishers, Inc., 2004.

Hippolytus. "The Extant Works and Fragments of Hippolytus." In *Ante-Nicene Fathers*, vol. 5. Peabody: Hendrickson Publishers, Inc., 2004.

Hurtado, Larry W. *At the Origins of Christian Worship*. Grand Rapids: Wm. B. Eerdmans Publishing Co., 2000.

Hurtado, Larry W. *Lord Jesus Christ*. Grand Rapids: Wm. B. Eerdmans Publishing Co., 2005.

Ignatius. "The Epistle of Ignatius to the Ephesians." In *Ante-Nicene Fathers*, vol. 1. Grand Rapids: WM. B. Eerdmans Publishing Co., 1996.

Ignatius. "The Epistle of Ignatius to the Magnesians." In *Ante-Nicene Fathers*, vol. 1. Grand Rapids: Wm B. Eerdmans Publishing Co. 1996.

Ignatius. "The Epistle of Ignatius to the Philadelphians." In *Ante-Nicene Fathers*, vol. 1. Grand Rapids: Wm. B. Eerdmans Publishing Co., 1996.

Ignatius. "The Epistle of Ignatius to Polycarp." In *Ante-Nicene Fathers*, vol. 1. Grand Rapids: Wm. B. Eerdmans Publishing Co., 1996.

Ignatius. "The Epistle of Ignatius to the Romans." In *Ante-Nicene Fathers*, vol. 1. Grand Rapids: Wm. B. Eerdmans Publishing Co., 1996.

Ignatius. "The Epistle of Ignatius to the Trallians." In *Ante-Nicene Fathers*, vol. 1. Grand Rapids: Wm. B. Eerdmans Publishing Co., 1996.

Irenaeus. "Fragments from the Lost Writings of Irenaeus." In *Ante-Nicene Fathers*, vol. 1. Grand Rapids: Wm. B. Eerdmans Publishing, Inc., 1996.

Irenaeus. "Irenaeus against Heresies." In *Ante-Nicene Fathers*, vol. 1. Grand Rapids: Wm. B. Eerdmans Publishing, Inc., 1996.

Kaku, Michio. *The Future of the Mind*. New York: Doubleday, 2014.

Kelly, J. N. D. *Early Christian Doctrines*. New York: Harper Collins Publishers, 1978.

Knight, George A. F. *Christ the Center*. Scotland: Handsel Press, and Grand Rapids: Wm. B. Eerdmans, 1999.

Knight, George W. *The Names of God*. Uhrichsville: Barbour Publishing, Inc., 2009.

Lactantius. "The Divine Institutes of the Origin of Error." In *Ante-Nicene Fathers*, vol. 7. Peabody: Hendrickson Publishers, Inc., 2004.

Lewis, C. S. *The Screwtape Letters*.

"Liturgy of James." In *Ante-Nicene Fathers*, vol. 7. Peabody: Hendrickson Publishers Inc., 2004.

MacGregor, Geddes. *Introduction to Religious Philosophy*. Boston: Houghton Mifflin Company, 1959.

Machen, J. Gresham. *Christianity and Liberalism*. Grand Rapids: Wm. B. Eerdmans Publishing Co., 1974.

Martyr, Justin. "Dialogue of Justin with Trypho, a Jew." In *Ante-Nicene Fathers*, vol. 1. Michigan: Wm. B. Eerdmans Publishing, Inc., 1996.

Martyr, Justin. "First Apology of Justin Martyr." In *Ante-Nicene Fathers*, vol. 1. Grand Rapids: Wm. B. Eerdmans Publishing Co., 1996.

Martyr, Justin. "Justin's Hortatory Address to the Greeks." In *Ante-Nicene Fathers*, vol. 1. Grand Rapids: Wm. B. Eerdmans Publishing Co., 1996.

Mathetes. "Epistle of Mathetes to Diognetus." In *Ante-Nicene Fathers*, vol. 1. Grand Rapids: Wm. B. Eerdmans Publishing, Co., 1996.

Mathetes. "Epistle to Diognetus." In *Ante-Nicene Fathers*, vol. 1. Grand Rapids: Wm. B. Eerdmans Publishing Co., 1996.

Methodius. "Oration Concerning Simeon and Anna." In *Ante-Nicene Fathers*, vol. 6. Peabody: Hendrickson Publishers Inc., 2004.

Methodius. "Oration on the Psalms." In *Ante-Nicene Fathers*, vol. 6. Peabody: Hendrickson Publishers Inc., 2004.

Novatian. "Treatise Concerning the Trinity." In *Ante-Nicene Fathers*, vol. 5. Peabody: Hendrickson Publishing Co., 2004.

Olson, Rodger E. and Christopher A. Hall. *The Trinity*. Grand Rapids: Wm. Eerdmans Publishing Co., 2002.

Origen. "Origen against Aelsus." In *Ante-Nicene Fathers*, vol. 4. Peabody: Hendrickson Publishers Inc., 2004.

Origen. "Origen against Celsus." In *Ante-Nicene Fathers*, vol. 4. Peabody: Hendrickson Publishers Inc., 2004.

Origen. "Origen's Commentary on the Gospel of John." In *Ante-Nicene Fathers*, vol. 9. Peabody: Hendrickson Publishers Inc., 2004.

Origen. "Origen De Principiis." In *Ante-Nicene Fathers*, vol. 4. Peabody: Hendrickson Publishers Inc., 2004.

Pearcey, Nancy. *Total Truth*. Illinois: Crossway Books, 2004.

Peter of Alexandria. "Fragments." In *Ante-Nicene Fathers*, vol. 6. Peabody: Hendrickson Publishers Inc., 2004.

Polycarp. "The Epistle of Polycarp to the Philippians." In *Ante-Nicene Fathers*, vol. 1. Grand Rapids: Wm. B. Eerdmans Publishing Co., 1996.

Pseudo-Clementine Literature. "Recognitions of Clement." In *Ante-Nicene Fathers*, vol. 8. Peabody: Hendrickson Publishers Inc., 2004.

Putnam, Robert D. *Bowling Alone*. New York: Simon & Schuster, 2000.

Raschke, Carl. *The Next Reformation*. Grand Rapids: Baker Academic, 2004.

Schaffer, Francis. *Genesis in Space and Time*, Downers Grove: InterVarsity Press, 1972.

Schaeffer, Francis. *How Should We Then Live?* New Jersey: Fleming H. Revell, 1967.

Schaeffer, Francis A. *The Church at the End of the 20th Century.* Wheaton: Crossway Books, 1985.

Schaffer, Francis A. *The Finished Work of Christ.* Wheaton: Crossway Books, 1998.

Schaffer, Francis A. *True Spirituality.* Carol Stream: Tyndale House Publishers, 2001.

Sire, James W. *The Universe Next Door.* Illinois: InterVarsity Press, 1997.

Spencer, Aida Besancon and William David Spencer, eds. *The Global God.* Grand Rapids: BridgePoint Books, 1998.

St. Athanasius. *On the Incarnation.* Crestwood: St. Vladimir's Seminary Press, 1977.

Tatian. "Tatian's Address to the Greeks." In *Ante-Nicene Fathers*, vol. 2. Peabody: Hendrickson Publishers Inc., 2004.

Tatian. "The Text of the Diatessaron." In *Ante-Nicene Fathers*, vol. 9. Peabody: Hendrickson Publishers Inc. 2004.

Tertullian. "Against Hermogenes." In *Ante-Nicene Fathers*, vol. 3. Grand Rapids: Wm. B. Eerdmans Publishing Co., 1986.

Tertullian. "Against Marcion." In *Ante-Nicene Fathers*, vol. 3. Grand Rapids: Wm. B. Eerdmans Publishing Co., 1986.

Tertullian. "Against Praxeas." In *Ante-Nicene Fathers*, vol. 3. Grand Rapids: Wm. B. Eerdmans Publishing Co., 1986.

Tertullian. "Tertullian on Prayer, Tertullian on Patience." In *Ante-Nicene Fathers*, vol. 3. Grand Rapids: Wm. B. Eerdmans Publishers Co., 1986.

Tertullian. "The Answer to the Jews." In *Ante-Nicene Fathers*, vol. 3. Grand Rapids: Wm. B. Eerdmans Publishers Co., 1986.

Tertullian. "The Apology." In *Ante-Nicene Fathers*, vol. 3. Grand Rapids: Wm. B. Eerdmans Publishers Co., 1986.

Tertullian. "The Prescription against Heretics." In *Ante-Nicene Fathers*, vol. 3. Grand Rapids: WM. B. Eerdmans Publishing Co., 1986.

Tertullian. "Treatise on the Soul." In *Ante-Nicene Fathers*, vol. 3. Peabody: Hendrickson Publishers Inc., 2004.

Thaumaturgus, Gregory. "Fourth Homily." In *Ante-Nicene Fathers*, vol. 6. Peabody: Hendrickson Publishers Inc., 2004.

Thaumaturgus, Gregory. "The Oration and Panegyric Addressed to Origen." In *Ante-Nicene Fathers*, vol. 6. Peabody: Hendrickson Publishers Inc., 2004.

Thaumaturgus, Gregory. "Twelve Topics on the Faith." In *Ante-Nicene Fathers*, vol. 6. Peabody: Hendrickson Publishers Inc., 2004.

Theophilus of Antioch. "Theophilus to Autolycus." In *Ante-Nicene Fathers*, vol. 2. Peabody: Hendrickson Publishing Co., 2004.

"The Testaments of the Twelve Patriarchs." In *Ante-Nicene Fathers*, vol. 8. Peabody: Hendrickson Publishers Inc., 2004.

Tatian. "Address of Tatian to the Greeks." In *Ante-Nicene Fathers*, vol. 2. Peabody: Hendrickson Publishers Inc., 2004.

Vanantius. "Poem on Easter." In *Ante-Nicene Fathers*, vol. 7. Peabody: Hendrickson Publishers Inc., 2004.

Victorinus. "Commentary on the Blessed John." In *Ante-Nicene Fathers*, vol. 7. Peabody: Hendrickson Publishers Inc., 2004.

Victorinus. "On the Creation of the World." In *Ante-Nicene Fathers*, vol. 7. Peabody: Hendrickson Publishers Inc., 2004.

Webster's New Collegiate Dictionary. Springfield: G. & C. Merriam Co., 1973.

Whiston, William. *Josephus*. Nashville: Thomas Nelson Publishers, 1998.

Wolf, Allen. *Transformation of American Religion*. New York: Free Press, 2003.

ABOUT THE AUTHOR

Michael F. Lawlor, born in Danbury, Connecticut. Attended Henry Abbot Technical School. Enlisted in the United States Army, 1964-1967. 1967-1973 various employment. 1973-1976 entered David Lipscomb Collage, earned B.A. in biblical studies. 1976-1981 Minister of the Churches of Christ. 1981-1982 Executive Director of the Pro-Life Council of Connecticut. Last employment Chief Executive of Colony Mortgage Inc. 1999 to present disabled.

Printed in the United States
By Bookmasters